"A veritable compendium of do  the street, at the veterinary cl about wherever dogs and peo Charlotte Reed convincingly e: the foremost authority of a c canine behavior and manners. Charlotte knows dogs, she knows people, and she knows how they fit together in every possible setting. A must read for everyone who has a dog, or hopes to someday."

—Donald F. Smith, DVM, dean,
College of Veterinary Medicine, Cornell University

"There are no bad dogs, only bad owners. It's not just a television sound bite; it's a fact. Today, with a great spiritual and emotional attachment to our dogs, we treat them as members of the family—we want to include them in everything we do and take them everywhere we go. Our dogs need to know what is expected of them—doggie etiquette—and it's your job, as a good owner, to teach them. Charlotte Reed's wonderful, entertaining, and practical book will help you train your dog to be a good citizen and a happy member of the family, at home or out in public."

—David Frei, cohost,
The Westminster Kennel Club Dog Show

"*Miss Fido Manners* is a wonderful resource for people who want their dogs to be welcomed with open doors at their favorite restaurants, hotels, and shops. For that matter, any dog owner who wants a pleasant canine companion should follow this guide. If you manage your dog's training, behavior, and grooming as Charlotte Reed prescribes, you'll enjoy each other's company more, and travel effortlessly through busy streets, veterinary clinics, your office, and even to the beach and ballpark."

—Susan Chaney, editor, *Dog Fancy* magazine

"Charlotte Reed has put together a very timely and ultimately useful book on a topic that has become increasingly important to pet owners and non-pet owners alike. As pets have become a more important part of our lives, it is up to all of us to be more conscious of the impact these companions have on the world around us. Charlotte takes a very practical approach to dealing with potentially uncomfortable situations. Coupled with some of the new and innovative products on the market today, the guidelines in this book will make owning a pet an even more rewarding experience."

—Bob Vetere, president,
American Pet Products Manufacturers Association

"This lovely book is so easy to read, to understand, and oh so helpful for doggie people (and those not so doggie). It will help you learn how to keep your friends and neighbors friendly and neighborly. Everyone needs this book."

—Mordecai Siegal, author,
Good Dog, Bad Dog and *The Cornell Book of Cats*

THE

Miss Fido Manners

COMPLETE BOOK *of* DOG ETIQUETTE

THE DEFINITIVE GUIDE *to* MANNERS *for* PETS *and* THEIR PEOPLE

Charlotte Reed

Adams Media
Avon, Massachusetts

Published by
Adams Media, an F+W Publications Company
57 Littlefield Street, Avon, MA 02322 U.S.A.
www.adamsmedia.com

ISBN-10: 1-59869-132-5
ISBN-13: 978-1-59869-132-0

Printed in the United States of America.

J I H G F E D C B A

Library of Congress Cataloging-in-Publication Data
Reed, Charlotte (Charlotte R.)
The Miss Fido manners complete book of
dog etiquette / by Charlotte Reed.
p. cm.
ISBN-13: 978-1-59869-132-0 (pbk.)
ISBN-10: 1-59869-132-5 (pbk.)
1. Dogs—Behavior. 2. Dogs—Training. I. Title.
SF433.R44 2007
636.7'0887–dc22
2007002722

This publication is designed to provide accurate and authoritative information
with regard to the subject matter covered. It is sold with the understanding that
the publisher is not engaged in rendering legal, accounting, or other professional
advice. If legal advice or other expert assistance is required, the services of a
competent professional person should be sought.
—From a Declaration of Principles jointly adopted by a Committee of the
American Bar Association and a Committee of Publishers and Associations

Many of the designations used by manufacturers and sellers to distinguish their
product are claimed as trademarks. Where those designations appear in this
book and Adams Media was aware of a trademark claim, the designations have
been printed with initial capital letters.

Interior illustrations by Tamaye Perry and ©iStockphoto.com/Jason Shadrick.

This book is available at quantity discounts for bulk purchases.
For information, please call 1-800-289-0963.

This book is dedicated to my parents, John and Eunice Reed. I thank them for their love and guidance. And to the Fabulous Baker Boys. Thank you very much for being great friends over the years!

Acknowledgments

I wish to acknowledge my A-Team: Editor Jennifer Kushnier, mentor Mordecai Siegal, friend Christopher Trela, advisor Beth Adelman, my jill of all trades, Nancy Zatzman, and agent, Peter Miller.

This book would have never happened without your support and confidence.

And I must not forget the original Two Dogs: This Goat thanks Katie and Kidder, the dogs that changed my life!

Contents

xi   Introduction

1 Part I ✎ AT-HOME PROPRIETY

2   Chapter 1 Good Manners Begin at Home
9   Chapter 2 Grooming and Dressing
21   Chapter 3 Dining at Home with Distinction
32   Chapter 4 Welcoming Guests to Your Home

43 Part II ✎ DECORUM WITH FAMILY, FRIENDS, AND STRANGERS

44   Chapter 5 A Guide to Canine-Child Interaction
50   Chapter 6 A Good-Neighbor Policy
65   Chapter 7 The Pawfect Pet Gift
71   Chapter 8 Proper Pet Party Planning
82   Chapter 9 Four-Legged Wedding Guests

89 Part III ✎ ETIQUETTE OUT AND ABOUT

90   Chapter 10 Street Smarts
103   Chapter 11 Best Practices at the Dog Run
109   Chapter 12 Pet Protocol in Retail Establishments
119   Chapter 13 Eating Out with Elegance
125   Chapter 14 Doggy Demeanor at the Office

133   Part IV ✐ PROTOCOL WITH PET
              PROFESSIONALS

134   Chapter 15 Vet Esteem
145   Chapter 16 Taking Care of Pet Nannies
152   Chapter 17 Being Gracious with Groomers
160   Chapter 18 Handling Dog Trainers Well
167   Chapter 19 Good Manners at Boarding Kennels

175   Part V ✐ TRAVEL, SPORTS, AND
              LEISURE

176   Chapter 20 Best Guest Behavior
182   Chapter 21 Traveling with Canine Panache
197   Chapter 22 Beach Dog Behavior
203   Chapter 23 Happy Trails
209   Chapter 24 Being a Good Sport at the Ballpark

217   Part VI ✐ GRACIOUSNESS IN THE
              WORST OF TIMES

218   Chapter 25 Dogs, Custody, and Divorce
224   Chapter 26 The Etiquette of Relinquishing
                       Your Pet
232   Chapter 27 Death, Burial Rituals, and
                       Commemorative Services

239   Epilogue
241   Index

Introduction

As the owner of Two Dogs & A Goat Incorporated, a leading pet-care service in New York City, I have taught clients how to behave in certain situations with their animals. Some customers have inquired about tipping practices for pet sitters, dog walkers, and groomers. One training client wanted me to teach her poodle how to eat at her favorite café on Madison Avenue. Another wanted me to show him how to run errands with his dog. I have even been asked to help relocated executives' families deal with difficult, non-pet-owning neighbors and to properly prepare a dog for a condo or co-op interview.

As a New York pet owner, I didn't find these situations unusual. Pet owners ask me for help because they love their dogs, treat them like family members, and want to share their lives with these companions. While learning how to teach their pets to behave, these pet parents are surprised to find that they themselves have acted inappropriately time and time again. It is in my private training sessions or in dog-training classes that they begin to understand that good manners have to be practiced at both ends of the leash.

Pet etiquette is the art of understanding and behaving properly with your companion. Whether we are with a pet-owning neighbor, at the veterinarian's office, or on the city streets, we dog owners have to be well-mannered and model citizens. This book is designed for that purpose alone. It will teach you to behave appropriately in all kinds of situations, making you a model pet owner, a good neighbor, an excellent customer, an exceptional host, and a welcome guest at the homes of friends and family. Specifically, you will learn how to apply conventional manners (consideration of others, good table manners, gift-giving, being a considerate guest, getting along with coworkers) to life with your dog.

The Miss Fido Manners Complete Book of Dog Etiquette is not a dog-training book. Instead, it explains why learning the right way to conduct yourself with your dog enables you to enjoy each other's company and share more of your life with your pet. As a socially aware pet owner, use this definitive guide as a finishing school primer for your dog.

Charlotte Reed

PART 1

At-Home Propriety

Chapter 1

Good Manners
BEGIN AT HOME

My mother believed in home training. She always said, "Good manners are learned at home." Mrs. Reed instilled in her children the knowledge that although making a favorable impression is something you have the opportunity to do only once, it is something that is done over and over again, everywhere you go. The same lesson can be applied to life with your pet.

FIRST STEPS FOR FIRST IMPRESSIONS

In order to make a good impression with your dog, you must follow all municipal rules pertaining to dog ownership—such as license, leash, rabies, pooper scooper laws—and only bring your dog where she is a welcome guest. Learn more about city dog laws in Chapter 10. For her to make a favorable appearance, she must be healthy, be well-groomed, have a calm demeanor, and be well-behaved.

To keep your pet healthy, schedule two appointments each year with her veterinarian: once in the fall and winter months for annual vaccinations and again in the spring to prepare for the summer and to protect her from fleas, ticks, and heartworm. If your dog does not have a microchip (an identification code implanted between the shoulder blades) as a second form of identification, discuss this with your vet at either one of these yearly examinations. Remember that a comprehensive annual examination followed by a later checkup provides a valuable benchmark for her health. We'll discuss vet appointments again in Chapter 15.

HOME GROOMING

Regular grooming contributes to good pet health, too. Although people gravitate toward a well-groomed dog, the benefits of grooming go far beyond a well-coifed furry face. Even if you take your pet to a professional groomer once a month, be sure to give her a good brushing and combing at least once a week to remove shedding hair and dirt from her coat, to keep your house clean, and to alleviate the pet dander for allergy sufferers in your home. Regular grooming also serves as a valuable tool for early illness detection because it allows you to become familiar with your pet's physique. During each grooming session, take time to familiarize yourself with your dog by gently stroking her entire body. With these routine

3

inspections, you're likely to notice abnormal growths, inflammations, or problem areas on her body. End each session with a quick examination of her face: check over her mouth, nose, ears, and eyes, being watchful for any unusual odors or discharges. Home grooming is covered more thoroughly in Chapter 2, and you'll find more about professional grooming in Chapter 17.

DIET

Keeping up your dog's appearance also involves being mindful of her diet. According to the National Research Council, one out of every four dogs in the western world is obese. Like humans, dogs that are overweight can develop diabetes, heart disease, or other health problems. To keep your dog fit, provide her with a nutritious meal twice a day and access to fresh, clean water all day long. If your dog is overweight, slim her down by feeding her smaller amounts of food or a low-calorie diet dog food, by refraining from feeding her table scraps, and by preventing her getting into trash cans.

EXERCISE

Diet and exercise go hand in hand to keep her looking good. Regular exercise is necessary to reduce an animal's stress and destructive behavior, control weight, and improve muscle tone, and it makes for a calm pet, too. Walking your dog a few times a day is the best consistent form of exercise, but vigorous play especially contributes to a healthy mind and a healthy body. Play with your dog according to her natural tendencies. For retrievers, there is nothing like a good game of fetch; for terriers who like to chase, have them run after the point of a laser light. Or take your dog swimming—there is a reason they call it the dog paddle. Dog runs and dog parks are other great places to help your animal companion burn off energy and socialize with her dog friends.

PET TIP

Other than providing pet health services, veterinarians are valuable resources when hiring pet professionals and recommending products to help you care for your pet.

TRAINING

Without a doubt, the key to having a well-mannered dog is dog training. Ask your veterinarian for a referral to a dog trainer or a dog-training facility. Working with a dog trainer is discussed in Chapter 18, but it is also a good idea to ask your vet to recommend a good training book that emphasizes a positive, not punitive, approach to dog training such as *Woman's Best Friend* by Babette Haggerty-Brennan, *Good Owners, Great Dogs* by Brian Kilcommons with Sarah Wilson, or *When Good Dogs Do*

5

Bad Things by Mordecai Siegal and Matthew Margolis. With or without professional help, your dog should learn to sit, stay, down, come, and heel. Most likely, she will train using the "bait and lure" methodology, in which she will learn commands, perform, and be rewarded with cookies. Eventually your dog will have to learn commands for the sake of her safety—and you will not always have dog treats in your pocket. Practicing all the commands on a daily basis ensures that they will soon be implemented into your and your dog's lives with ease. When walking, she will heel; when approaching the corner, she will sit; and at the dog park, she will come when called.

My client Emily followed these very steps with her terrier mix, Spike. Emily worked hard on Spike's training routine and, as a result, Spike was one of the most popular dogs in the neighborhood. Emily kept Spike healthy, clean, and well groomed, so no one would come away from petting him with fleas, dirty hands, or dog hair all over their clothes. Emily and Spike were inseparable—Emily even took him with her to work most days. He was also a welcome guest at shops along their route home. Spike walked by her side as she navigated the narrow aisles, and only greeted people when Emily gave him the "OK" signal. Many of the shop owners kept jars of doggy treats under the counter just for Spike's visits. Emily had also taught Spike to sit for petting, so neighbors could greet him in the elevator of her building without being jumped on.

Emily used the basic commands—Stay, Sit, Come, Heel—every day to give Spike clear instructions on how to behave, and gave equal consideration to her dog and to the people around her. Thanks to her thoughtfulness, Spike's outgoing nature was channeled into behavior that made him welcome wherever he and Emily went.

Having a healthy and well-trained dog like Spike will afford you more opportunities to share your life with your dog. You might be able to take her to your office; visit friends and family for a weekend; take a vacation with her; enjoy activities like hiking or going to other events, such as baseball games; and even have friends or family stay in your home. But in order to have a well-mannered dog, you need to provide her with a loving and structured environment—an environment that emphasizes that you and your dog are a team and are prepared to go anywhere.

PRODUCT RESOURCE GUIDE

Discuss flea, tick, and heartworm prevention with your vet. Interceptor is an oral tablet that prevents canine heartworm disease and controls roundworms, hookworms, and whipworms (*www.ah.novartis.com*).

Frontline Plus provides long-lasting control of fleas and ticks on your dog, as well as in your home. It is gentle enough to use on puppies eight weeks of age and is waterproof for thirty days (*www.frontline.com*).

HomeAgain Pet Recovery Service serves as a second form of identification other than a tag on a collar. The microchip is a pet retrieval system that is available from your veterinarian (*www.homeagainid.com*).

There's nothing like a good game of fetch on land or in the water. Try an Air Kong Squeaker, a tennis ball with a squeaker (*www.kongcompany.com*).

Consider these training books: *Woman's Best Friend* by Babettte Haggerty-Brennan (McGraw-Hill, 2003), *Good Owners, Great Dogs* by Brian Kilcommons with Sarah Wilson (Warner Books, 1999), and *When Good Dogs Do Bad Things* by Mordecai Siegal and Matthew Margolis (Little, Brown and Company, 1993).

The Laser Pet Toy is all about fun pet exercise. Move the light around and watch your pet keep chasing—but be careful not to shine it in your pet's eyes (*www.miraclebeam.com*).

Just make sure that if your pet is going to swim and/or water-retrieve, keep her safe in the water with a Canine Flotation Coat (*www.ruffwear.com*).

Chapter 2

Grooming AND *Dressing*

Personal appearance matters for you and your dog. Because keeping up appearances is a prerequisite to good manners, especially if you and your pooch are on the go, what matters most is how well he is groomed. If he is well groomed, it reflects not only how you treat your dog but also your awareness of those around you. So, just as you schedule a salon appointment for yourself, make a monthly appointment for him with a professional coiffeur (see Chapter 17). Between appointments, however, you yourself must ensure that your dog looks and feels his best.

To properly groom your pooch at home on a regular basis, start by cleaning his face. Breeds with facial skin folds (bloodhounds, Boston terriers, bulldogs, Neapolitan mastiffs, Pekingese, pugs, Shar-Peis, Shih Tzus) need to have their faces cleaned daily to prevent dermatitis. To do this, gently pull back their facial folds and clean the area with either a pet wipe or a cotton ball and a mild cleanser obtained from your veterinarian. A gentle cleaning can prevent dirt, dead skin, and bacteria from collecting in the folds and causing irritation, infection, and odor.

Next, use eye wipes or a dampened cotton ball to clean around his eyes. If there is any discharge, use a flea comb; the comb's teeth are close together so that any matter can be removed easily without causing your pet any discomfort. If the area under the eyes is discolored and wet from excessive tearing, as happens with breeds such as Maltese, poodles, bichon frisés, Old English sheepdogs, and Saint Bernards, keep the area as dry as possible to prevent bacteria or yeast infection. You can also use dog-safe stain-removing products to help reduce discoloration. When you clean his ears, use either an ear wipe or moistened cotton ball with ear cleanser to gently swab the inside of the ear flap. This is especially important for dogs like American cocker spaniels that have hanging ears, because their ear channels are obstructed, allowing bacteria to build up. For each ear, use a fresh piece, and be careful not to probe too deeply inside his ear canal.

MANICURES AND PEDICURES

If necessary, a pet master or mistress might have to become a pet manicurist. Your new profession can begin if you hear your dog's nails tapping on your wood or tile floors, signifying that his nails are much too long, or if you see that they are broken. Start by cleaning the dirt and debris with a moistened cotton pad between his toes. When trimming dog nails, select appropriately sized canine nail clippers. Take care to trim the nails without cutting the quick, or the blood supply. The quick is easier to see in pale nails, and very difficult with darker ones. For a dog with pale nails, clip nails almost up the blood supply; for dogs with dark nails, try and determine the location of the quick by examining the underside of the nail.

PET TIP

To make it easier to find everything, keep all of your grooming supplies together in one bag.

On darker nails, the area that should be clipped appears lifeless or dead with a whitish hue. As you continue to clip, the quick area will darken. Always clip the nail from the underside at a 45-degree angle, making a decisive, clean cut. Eventually, the quick will shrink back as you establish a monthly nail cutting routine. Before undertaking the task of a clipping a dog's nails, have a styptic on hand—just in case—to stop the bleeding if you cut too much. It is a good idea to have your veterinarian or groomer demonstrate how to perform this task before undertaking it.

BODY MAINTENANCE

Now that you've gotten the face and nails cleaned, move on to your dog's body. A brush and a comb are the easiest way to make him presentable in a relatively short amount of time. Use a bristle brush for short-coated breeds like beagles, a pin brush for long-coated breeds like Afghan hounds, and/or a slicker brush for long-coated breeds and for dogs that need to have their coats de-matted. Keep in mind that a good brushing is always followed by a combing, in order to remove any tangles or mats still left in your dog's coat.

One breed of dog that needs a lot of grooming (that can't necessarily be done at home) is a poodle. Caine, a standard poodle that lived in my friend Patti's Boston neighborhood, was in desperate need of grooming. His white hair was gray and tangled, and the hair around his mouth, eyes, and paws was stained. Every time Patti came across him with his owner, Caine was scratching and appeared dirty and uncomfortable. Once when she asked the owner if he was trying to "cord" the poodle's hair, he asked, "What's cording?" (Cording is very similar to the managed dreadlocks that Puli and Komondor dogs wear.) The owner didn't take the hint that she was referring to his completely matted dog with the filthy fur. So, one day Patti followed Caine and his owner home in order to obtain their address. For Christmas, Patti sent the dog coupons for a year's worth of dog grooming at a local grooming shop. Now when she sees the poodle, he looks regal, happier, and much healthier. She feels better, too!

A DOG IN THE TUB

If you are up to the challenge, you can also bathe your dog once a month, or as needed. Bathing not only helps to keep him clean and healthy, it also keeps your home clean and healthy. You'll find it is much easier to acclimate your pet to a regular grooming regime by starting when he is a puppy. Before bathing him, always brush and comb your dog thoroughly; trying to untangle wet, matted hair can be very difficult for you and uncomfortable for him.

Before you put your dog in the tub or sink, have the following supplies ready: cotton balls, pet shampoo and conditioner, a hose attachment, and two towels. You should use a rubber mat to avoid having your dog slip and injure himself, and have him on a leash and collar so that he is less likely to jump out of the tub or sink, creating an even messier situation!

To begin, use cotton balls to plug your pet's ears. Next, wet the coat with warm water. Instead of rubbing in circles, massage or knead the shampoo into a lather to avoid tangling your pet's hair, and pay attention to thoroughly washing the ears, rectal area, and feet. Shampoo your pet's head last, being very careful not to get the shampoo into his eyes, ears, or nose. Wash twice and rinse thoroughly three or four times, making sure to remove all the shampoo. When you condition your pet's coat with cream rinse, always rinse thoroughly.

When you are done bathing him, gently squeeze the fur all over his body to remove the excess water, then towel-dry him by blotting the coat. Comb and brush his fur again to make sure there are no tangles or mats left. If you wish, finish the job by using a blow dryer on a warm setting.

HEALTHY TEETH AND GUMS

Finally, it is time for his teeth. Although we have all heard jokes about doggy breath, nothing is worse than having a friendly dog with bad breath try to kiss your face. Yuck! Please, at least for the sake of preserving his social status, maintain your pet's healthy teeth and gums.

Like humans, dogs can suffer from dental problems. Food particles, bacteria, and debris can build up and harden on the surface of the teeth and the gums to form plaque. If unclean teeth are left unattended, severe infection, pain, and tooth loss can occur. The only way to prevent pet dental problems is to take care of your pet's mouth on a consistent basis. This is especially important for small dogs that usually are not big chewers, eat more canned food in their diets, have crowded teeth due to brachycephalic facial anatomy (like a Shih Tzu's), or have a tendency to retain baby teeth (like Yorkshire terriers).

Brush your dog's teeth regularly, preferably once a day, but at least once a week. Use a toothbrush designed specifically for pets, because it is smaller and softer, and never use human toothpaste because it contains ingredients that can make your pet sick if swallowed. To orchestrate a good brushing, sit him down in front of you after he has eaten dinner. Relax him by petting him and speaking to him in a calm voice, then carefully lift up or pull down his lip and gently brush along the teeth and gum line with appropriate pet dental products. Continue to brush the front, back, and top surfaces of all his teeth. Praise him when you are finished and treat him with some playtime.

Routine grooming is necessary not only for making your dog look his best and making a good impression, but for maintaining good health, too.

DOG FASHION

If you are going to dress your dog fashionably—and I'm talking beyond bandanas—make sure that he is dressed to impress with clean and spotless clothing. Build a pet wardrobe as you would build your own, with the practical, the stylish, and the outrageous. A smart way to keep some of your pet fashions looking their best is to hang items in a wardrobe on small hangers or place all articles of clothing in a custom-made pet armoire.

MISS FIDO MANNERS ON . . .

Caring for Pet Fashions

Before you buy doggy clothing, look at the care instructions. Wool, cashmere, and other specialty fabrics need to be dry-cleaned. Some clothes can be machine- or hand-washed but should be air-dried to avoid shrinkage. Use gentle cleaners, like Woolite, for special garments. Wash all pet clothing on the delicate cycle in garment bags.

Coats: Overcoats, more than any article of dog clothing, reflect popular human fashion. Whether your dog is wearing a velvet topper, a motorcycle jacket, or a sporty parka, it is more than likely designed as a "me-too" or made similar to a human fashion product. A dog's wardrobe should contain at least three coats: a winter parka, a light spring jacket, and a raincoat. When in seasonal use, dog coats should be cleaned on a regular basis. Remember, your dog is low to the ground and his clothing will get soiled very easily, especially on the melting snow days of winter or the rainy days of spring. Jackets made of leather or any other high-fashion fabric need specialty care. Do not hesitate to call the manufacturer and ask how best to take care of these items. To preserve their shape and prevent them from wrinkling, hang coats.

Sweaters: Sweaters are an excellent building block in any pet wardrobe and can be purchased at pet stores as well as fine boutiques. Although you can splurge on a cashmere or fine wool sweater for Fido, don't forget the additional dry-cleaning bills that come with it. Each season, purchase a few attractive, inexpensive pullovers for daily use. Sweaters are great additions to any wardrobe because they are worn close to the body and help retain body heat, which is essential, especially if you have a short-haired breed, senior dog, or young puppy. Sweaters are also nonconstricting outerwear that make it easier for dogs to play outside with their dog friends, because sweaters cannot be pulled off.

Leashes and collars: Even if your dog never wears clothing, he should always have at least one fashionable leash and collar. This effect can be achieved by purchasing an inexpensive nylon leash in a popular color, and by also having a leather leash and collar for special occasions. Many dog owners don't realize it, but leash and collar maintenance is absolutely necessary. Nylon leashes and collars should be washed in a garment bag to protect your washer and dryer from scratches and nicks. Leather leashes and collars can either be cleaned at home, like a good pair of shoes, or be taken to the shoe repairman for a good cleaning and polishing. Having your dog wear a dirty leash and collar is just a basic fashion faux pas.

T-shirts: As a fashion accessory, a dog and his owner can never have enough T-shirts. T-shirts come in various styles, from the Tuxedo Tee to the hip, urban graffiti-wear or the beautiful art wear adorned with Swarovski crystals. Just make sure your dog wears an appropriate tee for the proper occasion, and never dress him in a child's T-shirt, modified to ensure comfort or not.

Dresses: Having a dog wear a dress is a relatively new idea in dog fashion. To help them look their best, iron or dry-clean dresses so that they can maintain their fashion impact.

Haute Dog: When dogs are invited to fancy cocktail parties, elegant evening soirees, and other special occasions like weddings, it is fun to dress them in fine formalwear. For male dogs, purchase a tuxedo with all the trimmings including a cummerbund and top hat. Depending on the time of year, either wool or poly/cotton tuxes are available. Female dogs can look dazzling in gowns and cocktail dresses. Formalwear can be purchased at most pet boutiques or special-ordered from a doggy seamstress who make elegant outfits. Check the Web to find these doggy designers. As with all fancy clothing, dry-clean only and store in a garment bag to preserve the elegant look.

Boots: Boots are made for walking . . . in the snow and to protect paws from ice and salt. Although some pet owners—not me—like to accessorize their pet's feet with high-top fashion shoes, have him wear the shoes at home before wearing them out and about. If he doesn't, he may not be able to walk or he may lose one.

Jewelry: Accessorize a day or evening outfit with one piece of jewelry that is appropriate for the overall look. Have your dog wear a necklace, a hairclip, a bracelet, or magnetic earrings; wearing everything in the doggy jewelry box is gaudy and is definitely a doggy don't. Buy jewelry like you buy clothes. Make sure it fits comfortably and safely; find the appropriate size by measuring your pooch's neck and adding one inch. Exercise extreme caution with smaller pieces of jewelry such as earrings so that your dog doesn't swallow them and they don't fall into his ear canal. Also, to prevent damage to the hair and scalp, make sure hairclips are not worn too tight.

PRODUCT RESOURCE GUIDE

If you need to find a dog groomer in your community, visit *www.findagroomer.com*.

Petkin manufactures body, ear, eye, and facial wipes to keep your pet clean and healthy (*www.petkin.com*).

Eye Envy is a treatment solution to remove eye stains (*www.eyeenvy.com*).

Bamboo makes multipurpose grooming tools. Their three-in-one grooming products (brush and comb combinations) make it easy to coif your dog's coat. The three-in-one nail clipper comes with a styptic and file, both stored in the clipper handle (*www.bamboo pet.com*).

Use the FURminator, a de-shedding tool, to remove loose or dead hair on breeds that shed, like German shepherds (*www.furminator.com*).

When your dog is in need of a bath, try Bobbi Panter's Natural Pet Pampering Products. Bobbi has four shampoos and one detailing conditioner to deal with any fur-raising experiences. Whether your dog is itchy, stinky, or just having a bad hair day, Bobbi's products can make him simply gorgeous (*www.bobbipanter .com*).

To control plaque and fight bad breath, maintain your pet's mouth with Petrodex Toothpaste and Dental Rinse (*www.virbac.com*).

Although it is sold as a travel bag, I like to put all of my pet grooming supplies in a W.A.G. Bag (*www.ruffwear .com*).

Chapter 3

Dining AT HOME WITH *Distinction*

Just like children, our dogs should be taught good manners and proper behavior at mealtimes. A dog that steals from the kitchen counter could spoil any meal, especially when you are having a dinner party and her thievery has cost you the meal. A good meal can also be ruined by a begging, whining, or drooling dog at the table in the company of family or friends. Worse yet, imagine a dog that frightens you with her growling, snapping, and barking as you approach her while she is eating. These scenarios display canine behavior that is more than just rude—it is unacceptable in my house as much as it should be in yours.

Instill respectful habits in your dog by controlling her access to food and water. To achieve your pooch's best dining behavior, feed her twice a day, at the same time of day, for approximately twenty-minute intervals. By instructing her when and for how long she eats, you are confirming that you are responsible for her food intake. Also, feeding your dog on a consistent schedule contributes to a healthier dog. She'll have a regular constitution and will be less likely to steal or gorge on food, or have bloat—especially if she is a bigger dog, like a Great Dane, Saint Bernard, or Weimaraner.

THOU SHALT NOT STEAL

In most cases, dogs that steal food aren't being rude on purpose—they're just hungry. The smell of a fragrant meal permeating your home can make it difficult for a hungry dog to control herself. If you live with a doggy food thief, it is probably best not to leave a tasty rib roast or yummy plum tart on the kitchen counter or dining room table like my friend Nancy did.

Nancy thought that she had curbed her dachshund's food theft by instructing friends and family to pull their chairs far away from the table so that her Daisy would not climb up on the table and help herself to table scraps. However, during one holiday gathering at Nancy's Philadelphia home, she forgot to remind her niece of Daisy's bad habit. While Nancy was in the kitchen, the young girl arranged the silverware, pulled the chairs up to the table and put the platters and bowls filled with the holiday delights on the table. After her niece left the room to gather up the family, Daisy jumped onto the chair and then onto the table. As the family of twelve walked into the room, they were hushed by the sight of Daisy standing on the table feasting on the holiday meal. When she realized she had been caught, she looked them in the eye and barked as if to say, "A fine meal awaits you."

STOPPING THEFT

The simplest strategy for dealing with counter or table thievery such as Daisy's is to move food out of her reach, but if you have a big dog that can easily jump up on the kitchen counter or a dog that is just determined to get the food at all cost, you will have to make other provisions or set up booby traps in order to teach her better manners around mealtimes. Other than teaching eating manners, if you do leave food out on the counter or a table within a dog's reach, there is a good chance that your dog could help herself to the meal and perhaps get sick. Consequences such as having no meal to serve to dinner guests or having to pay a large vet bill for a satisfied but sick dog would inspire you to control this unpleasant behavior quickly.

As a first step to preventing or curbing theft, consider applying two-sided tape to the area—she probably won't like the feel of her paws sticking to the counter or a dining table. Another option is to set a closed can full of pennies on the edge of the counter that will fall as she jumps up. For persistent dogs, try an automatic pet deterrent, which will sound an alarm to warn her away from the counter. While some dogs respond to noise warnings like this, others do not. In extreme cases, you might have to utilize an electronic training tool by positioning a "scat mat" or training mat on the counter. When your pet touches the counter, the mat will give off a harmless shock, and she will learn to keep away from the area quite quickly.

Although these methods will cause your dog to realize that stealing food can produce an unpleasant consequence, my preferred method to curtail this activity is to deal with it the old-fashioned way. Train your dog to stay away from the kitchen counter—or even the table—if she steals food from there by teaching her to "Leave it." Start by getting two tasty treats or pieces of kibble; put one on the counter or tabletop and hide the other in your hand. Once she sees the food and moves toward it, tell her in a firm voice: "Leave it." Then cover the treat with your hand. Do not allow her to get the treat. When she does back off,

PET TIP

To make washing your feeding bowl easier, spray a little nonstick cooking oil in the bottom before you add the food. This works especially well if you are feeding your pet wet food, which has a tendency to dry out and stick to the bowl.

tell her that she is a "good girl." Wait a few seconds and repeat the exercise. When she backs off, give her the second treat, the one you've been hiding in your hand. Repeat this exercise a few times each day, in the kitchen or at the table, until your dog understands that she has to control herself and exercise good manners when you are cooking or preparing food at the counter, or even eating at the table. If she continues to appear hungry and can't control herself around food, schedule an appointment with your vet to discuss additional strategies, including changing her diet or determining whether she has a health problem.

FOOD AND WATERING BOWLS

All dogs should be given an age-appropriate and well-balanced diet, paired with fresh drinking water that should be changed a few times a day. Serve her meals and water in pet dinnerware made of stainless steel or ceramic, as these materials are easy to clean and can be placed in the dishwasher. For a puppy, choose an appropriate bowl for her size; for an adult or senior dog, use larger, raised bowls so she does not have to bend and stretch her neck. A dog that has a flat face, such as a Boston terrier, Lhasa apso, Pekingese, pug, or Shih Tzu, should be given a shallow bowl, so that if she is eating wet food she does not put her whole head in the bowl and stain her fur. For a dog with long ears, like a springer spaniel or basset hound, use a deep, narrow bowl to prevent dirty and food-stained ears.

All bowls should have skid-proof bottoms or should be heavy enough that dogs cannot move them while eating or drinking. As a cautionary note, check ceramic bowls on a regular basis for chipping and cracking. Bacteria can easily become lodged in the cracks and contaminate a pet's meal, and a chipped or cracked feeding bowl can also be a cutting hazard to a dog's face.

If your dog is a foodie who eats with such enthusiasm that her meal is often all over the floor, consider using a plastic placement. A matching placement creates the impression of a place setting, but more importantly, it can be wiped off over the garbage and can be rinsed easily.

ESTABLISH AN EATING ROUTINE

Avoid a feeding frenzy of jumping and crying for food by establishing a dining protocol when you bring a dog home for the first time. Before you serve her meal, command your dog to "Sit–Stay." Once she has done so and you have placed her dish in front of her, give her the "Okay" release command and let her eat. This way she will learn good manners during her mealtime as well as yours.

For a family of more than one dog, you will need to provide a controlled dining environment. Like little human beings, four-legged kids also like to play with their food and steal a meal from their siblings. Assign each dog a place to eat far enough away from the others so that they can all eat comfortably without worrying—thus preventing a flare-up of food-guarding instincts, which can lead to food-fighting. Have each dog leave the room when finished eating.

OVERPROTECTIVE EATERS AND MEALTIME AGGRESSION

If you have a dog who growls when you or another animal approaches her while she is eating, and you are afraid that she will bite the hand that feeds her (literally), you can call for professional help. A professional can evaluate your dog, devise a training regime, and recommend safety measures.

If, however, you prefer to take matters into your own hands, you can implement a counter-conditioning feeding program. Remember, your dog needs to understand that you choose when she eats and how she eats. To begin this feeding program, fill her bowl with pet food and hold the dish in your hands, rather than setting it on the floor. Have your dog "Come" to you and "Eat" from your hand on command. For each morsel of food, step away from her so that she has to "Come" to you for each bite of her food. Each time she comes and eats, praise her in a calm voice for being a "good dog." After she gets used to eating from your hand, you can eventually place the dish on the floor, but have her continue to eat from your hand on command. Gradually, you should be able to move the hand with the food closer to the dish for successive bites of food. Eventually, have her eat from your hand in the dish and, finally, have her eat from the dish while your hand is in it.

Next, it's important to implement exercises to make her feel secure about you approaching her while she is eating. Put the empty food dish down in her regular eating spot and walk away from the bowl. When the dog walks up to the dish and realizes that there is no food in the dish, tell her to "Sit." Walk over to the bowl and drop a few morsels of kibble in the bowl, then release her with the "Okay" command and tell her to "Eat." Always verbally praise her for following your instructions. After she finishes the small portion of kibble, continue to repeat the exercise. After a few attempts, command her to "Sit," walk over to the bowl and reward with petting instead of food. Continue rewarding her good behavior with food and/or petting. Once she feels comfortable having you come toward her food bowl, have family and friends attempt these exercises, too.

Take the rehabilitation program slowly. If you have difficulty moving forward, reinforce the previous step again. If you feel that your situation is not improving or is getting worse, do not punish your dog (because it is entirely possible that you accidentally created the problem), but call for professional help.

BEGGING FOR IT

Another bad behavior problem that always seems to develop from the best of intentions is table begging. From the day that she enters your home, never feed your dog from the table. Also, when guests arrive in your home, instruct them not to feed your dog. Explain to your guests how important it is for you to have a well-trained dog, especially around the dinner table, and if they feed her it could detract from her training. If that doesn't work, tell them that she is on a very strict diet, and even a slight disruption will cause her to have mishaps—more than likely, in the guest room. If you have a beggar girl on your hands, there is no need to ban her from the dining room: you can use a dog bed as a training tool to improve her bad manners. When your dog begs, tell her to "Leave it" and place her in a "Sit–Stay" on her bed. Each time she leaves the bed, tell her "No!" and have her return to her bed. Again, command her to "Sit–Stay" on her place. It is not going to be easy, and a few of your meals will probably get cold before she understands that she cannot beg for food. But persistence will pay off, and she will learn she must have good manners at your mealtimes, too. Eventually, you can remove the dog bed, but recognize that it gives her a comfortable place to lie down that is away from your dining table. If you do want to keep her bed in the dining room, consider having a bed or bed cover made in the fabric of your dining room drapes or tablecloth.

Practice good canine manners at all mealtimes each day. When these are used routinely, you will not have to worry about the emergence of bad doggy behavior whether you are eating alone, having guests over at your home, or feeding her daily meals.

PRODUCT RESOURCE GUIDE

To find a modern designed pet feeding bowl made of stainless steel, visit the Wetnoz Web site (*www.wetnoz.com*).

Castlemere makes whimsical ceramic bowls with pet-themed designs (*www.castlemere.com*).

Originally designed for felines, Sticky Paw! For Furniture are transparent adhesive strips that can easily be applied to countertops or table tops to prevent dogs from being where they shouldn't. The strips won't leave a sticky residue when they are removed (*www .stickypaws.com*).

Another pet deterrent is the automatic StayAway. When your dog approaches the area, the StayAway responds with a warning sound and/or a brief, harmless spray of compressed air (*www.contech-inc.com*).

If you need an animal behavior counselor, get in touch with the International Association of Animal Behavior Consultants, Inc. (*www.iaabc.org*) or The Association of Companion Animal Behavior Counselors (*www .animalbehaviorcounselors.org*).

Chapter 4

Welcoming Guests
TO YOUR HOME

Especially during the holidays, having friends or family come for a visit gives you the opportunity to enjoy time with loved ones. Whether you have a social, outgoing puppy or a shy, fearful dog, being a pet-owning host can be difficult. As a dog owner and host, you need to keep your dog at ease and your houseguest comfortable.

PREPARING FOR HOUSEGUESTS

In order to make the visit to your home as stress-free as possible, before your guests arrive, discuss your dog with them. Ask invitees if they suffer from dog allergies. The National Institute of Environmental Health Sciences and the U.S. Department of Housing and Urban Development conducted a national survey to measure levels of indoor allergens that might trigger asthma. They found that in homes with dogs, the levels of allergens were high enough that they could trigger allergies or asthma. People with dog allergies are generally sensitive to dog dander, saliva, and urine, so if your friends or family are allergic but still prefer to stay at your home instead of a hotel, discuss how to best alleviate their sensitivities.

Grooming your dog is one effective solution to reducing allergens. Shampoos and dips found at your local pet store can help reduce shedding and dander, but you should also address the already-shed dander by cleaning your home thoroughly. Another way to limit airborne allergens is to use a high efficiency particulate air (HEPA) filter. Studies have shown HEPA filters can reduce the amount of dog allergens in the air. Clinical studies do not prove that the use of HEPA filters can result in a reduction of medication; encourage your guests to discuss increasing the dose of their allergy medications with their physicians. The best defense for allergy sufferers is to keep your dog out of the guest room.

Next, talk about your pet's personality and behavior. If your dog is overly friendly and jumps on visitors or barks or growls at strangers, tell them to expect this, but be careful not to frighten them. Point out that while they are staying in your home it is important to maintain your dog's routine and that disruptions to his schedule can cause him anxiety or stomach upset or aggravate an illness. Ask them to be patient with your pooch and allow him to make friends on his own terms rather than forcing a relationship. Remind them that once they arrive at your home, you will need a few extra minutes to review all the dog-specific details.

GETTING YOUR DOG READY FOR VISITORS

Now that you have introduced your visitors to your pet's personality, it's time to prepare your dog for the houseguests.

If your dog is very happy to have visitors come to your home and demonstrates his enthusiasm for greeting people by jumping, he needs to be trained to keep his paws on the ground. Besides, who wants to create a bad impression with houseguests by frightening them or by having your dog jump and dirty their clothing. When he jumps up, train your dog by telling him "No!" and provide him with an alternative behavior. Request that he "Sit–Stay" and reward him for his good behavior with a "Good boy" in a calm and soothing voice. Furthermore, when the doorbell rings, put him on a leash before opening the door, and command him to "Sit–Stay." Should he jump up, pull down on his leash. If he continues to jump up, start the process again. And most importantly, don't let anyone, including houseguests, encourage his jumping or disruption of your training regimen. Explain to them that your consistent actions and loving manner help him keep his paws where they belong—down on the floor—and will eventually produce your desired result: a better trained dog!

A dog that has grown up having limited experience with people other than you might be apprehensive of visitors. Although it is best for a puppy or young adult dog to be socialized to visitors early on, some dogs do not have the opportunity. If you believe he will have any serious behavioral problems while you are having guests, ask your veterinarian or animal behavior counselor for help. In some cases, you may need to speak to your veterinarian about prescribing an anxiety-reducing medication or remedy to help reduce your dog's stress. Most of these medications take a few weeks to work effectively, so once you know the date of your guests' arrival, schedule an appointment with your vet immediately. Even if the veterinarian doesn't recommend pharmaceuticals, he may suggest other alternatives to ease your dog's anxiety, such as a pheromone wall plug-in or homeopathic remedy to comfort dogs in stressful situations.

Other than medication or alternative remedies, animal behavior counselors recommend that the best way to reduce your dog's stress is to create a retreat for him. If he normally relaxes in the living room or the room that your guests will occupy, relocate his bed and toys to your bedroom, or a room that is off-limits to houseguests.

It is unfortunate that Sallie, a Collie, did not have a spot like this when family visited her home for the Christmas holiday. When her owners, Lindsay and Kevin, decided to host their families, they were a bit anxious about having such a large crowd come to visit for a week. What they weren't worried about was their people-friendly Sallie, who had always been outgoing when having visitors in the past. Because they lived in a two-bedroom Manhattan apartment, they organized room accommodations at a nearby hotel so that both families would be within walking distance. On any given day no less than thirty people and five children were in and out of the apartment at various times of the day and night. Although Sallie was quite fond of people and liked children, she appreciated her space, peace, and quiet. After a few days, Lindsay and Kevin found her trying to hide under the bed, camping out in the closet, or relaxing in the bathtub. The crowded bustling apartment became too much for her to handle, so Sallie began to lie waiting by the front door hoping that someone would open it for her. Her persistence paid off when someone left the door ajar. Just by chance, the elevator door was open on her floor and she rode down to the basement.

Around eight o'clock the next morning, Kevin prepared Sallie's meal, assuming Sallie was still sleeping after all the excitement from the night before, and left it on the kitchen floor. The family went out to breakfast and when they returned, they noticed that the dog's meal hadn't been eaten and that Sallie was not in the apartment. After a few hysterical phone calls to the superintendent and building staff, disturbing their Christmas Day, the family of thirty mobilized within the apartment building. Within two hours, Sallie was found in the laundry room enjoying her much needed quiet time—and just in time to open holiday presents.

SOCIALIZING AND REHABILITATING YOUR DOG

Although Sallie had been an outgoing dog, the number of visitors had been too much even for her to handle. If your dog is shy or fearful to begin with, you will need to help him overcome his fear of strangers using principles of desensitization and counter-conditioning. Weeks before guests are due to arrive, ask other friends and neighbors to help you socialize your dog to strangers.

Before beginning mini-training sessions, remember that, at any time, your dog should always be able to retreat to another room. To get started acclimating your dog to others, have visitors come to your home and ignore him. Once inside, they should not look at, talk to, or try to touch your dog. After a few minutes of visiting with you, have them throw his favorite, or a very desirable, treat in the middle of the floor (to ensure your dog's interest in the treats, remove his food bowl a few hours before visitors arrive or substitute these treats for his dinner). If the dog comes out and takes the treat, have your houseguest toss another, a few inches short of the first. Repeat the process a few times, each time throwing the treat a shorter distance. Never force him, but allow your pet to take his time and make new friends at his own pace.

Continue the training exercises by having different friends and acquaintances come to your home each week, gradually increasing the length of their visits. The goal of these training sessions is to help your dog relax with strangers, associate benefits from their visits, and build his confidence. Recognize that it could take weeks, months, or longer for him to feel confident with friends or family in your home. If he doesn't show social improvement, you might have to keep your pet separated from houseguests. If you anticipate having a very difficult time, call a nearby kennel and book him for a visit;

PET TIP

With family and friends visiting, it is important to keep your pet on his regular feeding, walking, and sleeping schedule. If you are worried that you will not be able to maintain his schedule, hire a dog walker who can spend time with him and give him some special attention while you are hosting guests.

then you can take a break from your guests and visit with him there every day.

MEASURES GUESTS CAN TAKE

When guests arrive, explain what measures you have taken to help your dog overcome his fear of strangers, and ask them to do the same exercise your visiting friends have done over the last few weeks by placing kibble or a treat on the floor. Advise them to avoid feeding your dog table scraps, giving him human snacks, or engaging in activities that will rile him up. Also, tell guests to keep medications, toiletries, and other harmful items out of your dog's reach. Most importantly, ask them not to challenge your dog by staring at him, standing over him, or speaking loudly. Explain to them that if your dog approaches them, they should never approach him with an outstretched hand as if to pet his head because this action could make a dog feel threatened. Rather, they should allow him to sniff their hand. If the dog grants permission, they can then pet him gently under the chin.

Also, politely ask them to keep the door to the guest room closed at all times and to exercise extreme caution when leaving and entering your residence so that your dog does not, like Sallie in the story, slip out without appropriate supervision.

If children older than five years old are staying in your home, simply explain to them with their parents present that dogs do not always make good friends, and that they are to leave the dog alone, especially when he is sleeping, eating, or playing with his toys, unless the dog decides to play with them. Tell children to refrain from teasing, throwing things, playing rough games, or wrestling, because these behaviors may make your dog feel threatened and, as result, he could scare and bite them. Make it clear that they are never to sneak your pet food because it can make him sick. Insist that parents help you enforce your pet policy by always supervising children and your dog's interaction while the two are together. And if a toddler is staying in your home, don't just rely on his parents to watch him—put a baby gate at the entrance to your dog's retreat so that the child will leave your dog alone (and vice versa).

Even though you have guests, try to spend some time alone with your animal to help him keep his normal routine. To further relax him, take him out for a few long walks each day, play together with his toys, and pet and massage him.

Having friends or family come for a visit can be difficult when you have a dog. But if you take the time to describe your dog's personality and prepare your dog for houseguests, you will have an easier time balancing the needs of both of them. And then you will have a less stressful time, too!

PRODUCT RESOURCE GUIDE

To remove hair, dirt, and debris from your home, I suggest using the Dyson Animal Vac DC15. This upright vacuum is one of the few products that I can't live without (*www.dyson.com*).

Treat your pet with Allerpet to cleanse the hair of dander, saliva, and sebaceous-gland secretions and to reduce people's allergic reactions to dogs (*www .allerpet.com*).

To deactivate allergens in your home, spray the water-based solution Febreze on your pet's favorite resting spots (*www.febreze.com*).

Comfort Zone with D.A.P. (Dog Appeasing Phero-mones) helps to reduce pet stress. D.A.P. mimics a natural comforting pheromone produced by nursing dog mothers and helps settle pets down (*www.pet comfortzone.com*).

An alternative to relieve anxiety is Rescue Remedy, from Bach Flower Essences, available at most health food stores (*www.nelsonbach.com*).

For quiet time, give him a home of his own. Purchase a kennel for your pet at *www.midwesthomes4pets .com*.

PART II

Decorum with Family, Friends, and Strangers

Chapter 5

A Guide to CANINE-CHILD INTERACTION

Although your dog may be your baby and you spend your days and nights hugging her, kissing her, and telling her that she is a "Good girl," don't forget that your pet is an animal that can surprise you at a moment's notice with unexpected, and sometimes bad, behavior. If you see an enthusiastic child making a beeline toward you and your poochie, you need to think fast and take charge. As a responsible dog owner and adult, you will need to manage the behavioral interaction between the child and your dog to make certain that the two are well-behaved and know how to treat each other with respect.

SHOW CHILDREN HOW TO RESPOND

According to the National Center for Injury Prevention and Control, dog-bite injuries are highest for children between the ages of five and nine years old, and injury rates in children are significantly higher for boys than for girls. As a result, when dealing with children it is important to rely on your training repertoire to control your dog's behavior. When with youngsters, she must "Sit–Stay" to meet children, "Come" to you for safety's sake, and "Let's go" to avoid conflict.

If your dog is to make the acquaintance of youngsters, you must be very careful how you handle the situation. Children need to understand that, no matter how cute a dog looks or how fun she seems, dogs do not always make good friends. To have the best experience when interacting with dogs, children need to rely on adult direction.

Teach children how important it is that they be polite, for safety's sake, with dog owners and their pets. Instruct them to always ask if a dog is friendly and then if they may pet it. As well as acting graciously with dog owners, they must learn how to interact positively with dogs. When you run into children while walking your dog, it is always best to "show and tell" them how to greet your dog. When a child is introduced to her, your dog should be commanded to "Sit–Stay," and you should tell the youngster to be calm, lower his voice, and hold out a steady hand so that your dog can sniff it. Show the child first, and then have her mimic your actions.

If at any time your dog barks or seems to balk, terminate the meet-and-greet session by telling your dog to "Leave it." Without hurting the child's feelings, explain that your dog is not used to being around smaller people and doesn't feel comfortable. If your dog accepts his advances, tell him not to approach her with an outstretched hand, as if to pet her head, because this could make her feel threatened. Instead, he should pet under her chin first so that the dog will be able to relax and get to know him.

PET TIP

Ask parents to help you promote cordial and safe relations between your dog and their children by supervising children and enforcing appropriate behavior around your dog.

Many children will get extremely excited about meeting your dog and will want to try to treat her like a stuffed animal or make friends too quickly. Discourage them from trying to hug or cuddle your dog; instead, teach them how dogs communicate and what the best way is to communicate with yours.

TEACH KIDS TO COMMUNICATE

Tell kids that they need to understand the "secret" language of dogs by reading a dog's body. If they do not understand the concept of body language, explain it like this. When you are happy, you smile. When you are sad, you cry. Without words, your body reacts and shows how you feel—just like a dog's body can demonstrate how he feels. Explain that a friendly and content dog will paw their clothes or lick their hands as a sign of wanting more petting and attention. A frightened dog may back up, fall to the ground, shake from fear, urinate, pant, and even tilt her ears back; an angry dog may make herself appear bigger with erect ears and hair raised on the back of her neck and tail. An angry dog might also show her teeth and bark or growl to scare them so that they will leave her alone.

Because children have the best intentions, warn them that they should neither try to comfort the fearful dog nor challenge the angry one. Tell them that the best strategy is to remain silent, look away from the animal, and leave by walking away from the dog slowly.

Furthermore, let kids know that, believe it or not, dogs don't like surprises, and it is in their best interest not to disturb a dog that is sleeping, eating, or playing with her toys. Also, dissuade them from running wildly, screaming, or playing on the ground in the presence of a dog, because these behaviors could cause her to become riled up, to chase them, or to feel threatened—and, as result, scare and bite them.

More so with boys than girls, tell them not to tease, throw things, play rough games, or wrestle with your dog. And most importantly, neither boys nor girls should ever sneak your pet food. Tell them that once they make friends, she will like them just fine without them feeding her snacks or food, which could make her sick.

ALLOW OLDER CHILDREN TO HELP TRAIN

Unlike smaller children, older children might enjoy taking part in the training process. Teach them how to make your dog "Sit–Stay," and show them how to your walk your dog on a lead.

Children and dogs should only interact under the watchful eye of adults. To forge successful relationships, practice your dog-training skills and take advantage of opportunities where your dog will meet youngsters of all ages.

Jody, a dog owner with no children, decided that she would bring her three-year-old beagle, Darby, home for the holidays. Her mother was excited to host Darby, but was a bit concerned because her son's young children were also coming for the holidays. Jody assured her that Darby was very well socialized, but more importantly, he was well-trained. Before arriving with Darby for the holidays, she called her brother to discuss how everyone could have a successful holiday weekend by teaching the kids how to treat Darby and taking turns supervising the children with him. Because the weekend went off without a hitch, the following week her brother called for the name of Darby's breeder. He told Jody that after doing some research, he and his wife thought a beagle would be perfect for their two children.

PRODUCT RESOURCE GUIDE

To learn about dog-bite prevention for children, visit The Humane Society of the United States (*www.hsus.org*). They have a series of articles online and a coloring page for kids titled "Dog Bites Dos and Don'ts" that can be downloaded.

The National Association for Humane and Environmental Education has great gifts to introduce kids to dogs (*www.nahee.org*).

The third of May is National Dog Bite Prevention Week, and the American Veterinary Medical Association, the United States Postal Service, and the Centers for Disease Control and Prevention work to educate Americans about dog bite prevention. Visit the National Center for Injury Prevention and Control at the Centers for Disease Control and Prevention Web site (*www.cdc.gov*).

For kids ages nine through twelve, purchase *Dog Training for Kids* by Carol Lea Benjamin (Howell Book House, 2nd ed., 1998). The book teaches tweens basic dog obedience skills.

Chapter 6

A *Good-Neighbor* POLICY

The rules of canine etiquette extend far beyond the home and out into the neighborhood and community. Recognize that your behavior, and that of your pet, can affect your neighbors whether you live in an apartment, a condominium, or a house. By abiding by the pet regulations of a municipality and/or residential community, controlling your dog, practicing consideration, and promoting cordial relations, you can be an exemplary neighbor.

FOLLOW THE RULES

Before moving into a community and/or residential building, learn the pet rules and regulations, and use these to guide your behavior with your pooch. Most towns have licensing, leashing, and pooper-scooper laws, and some cities even have breed-specific statutes or regulations banning certain breeds (e.g., pit bulls, rottweilers, Doberman pinschers) to restrict or prohibit breeds that municipalities define as dangerous. Additionally, in certain living environments there are canine size restrictions (e.g., dogs up to twenty pounds allowed), designated walking areas, limits on the number of dogs per household, and facility mandates such as pet-appropriate elevators, exits, and entrances. Abide by these rules and you will limit your exposure to any canine troubles such as fines, terminated leases, and court appearances with their burdensome costs.

KEEPING YOUR PET UNDER CONTROL

Even if you follow the local laws and your dog appears to be as good as Lassie by day, don't let him transform into Cujo of the Hood at night. Many suburban homeowners complain that their pet-owning neighbors do not control their dogs, allowing them to roam in neighborhoods, urinate and defecate on lawns, dig holes under fencing, rummage through garbage cans, and bark at all hours.

So, if you are the owner of a Roaming Romeo or a Loose Lucy, first neuter or spay your dog to thwart his or her desire to search out the companionship of the opposite sex. Although it may cost a few dollars—whoever said having a modern dog was cheap?—install electric pet barriers, repair your fencing, or build a pet enclosure so that your dog can stay at home on your property. If he is confined in your backyard, he is less likely to impose upon your neighbors by pooping on their lawn or feasting on leftovers thrown in their garbage cans. By keeping your pet at home, you are also protecting him from wild animals, such as hungry coyotes that have been known to snatch dogs in the blink of an eye; preventing him from getting hit by car; or even averting a chance meeting with an animal abuser.

For those dog owners who have a serious digger on their hands, you must redirect his excavating fervor away from the fence. Be advised that dogs dig for a variety of reasons: to exercise, to create a cooling pit, to entertain themselves, or, in some cases, just to escape. Whatever the reason for his digging, you can supply him with his own quarry. Buy a hard plastic baby pool, fill it with sand, and hide toys and treats in it. This measure will encourage him to dig in the appropriate place, and he can be rewarded for his appropriate behavior. It also might make him enjoy and appreciate his home turf a bit more.

SUBURBAN NEIGHBORLY LOVE

Even though you've grounded him, you must continue to be considerate of your neighbors by cleaning up your own yard. Left to accumulate, dog waste attracts disease-carrying pests, can pollute groundwater sources, and offends your neighbors. Best to keep your yard clean, or get help from a professional pooper scooper, especially in the summer months when neighbors are spending more time outside and can be easily offended by the smell of your soiled yard. And always, always, always pick up after your pet in public places.

The Johnstons were a family that rarely cleaned up the waste of their three German shepherds in their own backyard. Because of the smell and the flies that plagued their gardens, the Johnstons' neighbors devised a plan that they hoped would give them a hint to clean up their yard. One evening, the Johnstons received a visit from a professional pooper scooper. Mrs. Johnston was surprised that the young man had a scheduled appointment, because she never scheduled a consultation. She thanked him for his time but told him that a mistake had been made. A few weeks later, the same young man visited again and explained that his office was called, an appointment was booked, and reconfirmed. He even mentioned her three German shepherds, which were out of sight. Once again, she turned him away. On the third visit, Mr. Johnson came to the door and told the young man to "stop soliciting or he would call the police." The young man remarked, "Perhaps your neighbors are trying to tell you something." Don't let your situation get this far out of hand: clean your yard as you would want your neighbors to clean theirs.

CITY DOGS

Suburbanites are not alone in complaining about neighbor dogs' bad behavior. City folk whine about what pet owners don't do. They blame filthy or poorly behaved dogs on the neglectful owners. In recent years dog ownership has grown, especially in metropolitan cities, and as a result humans and dogs live in close proximity, sharing apartment corridors, elevators, and lobbies. Apartment dwellers neither want to look at nor smell a dirty dog, nor be jumped upon by an untrained one. The most inexcusable behavior is a tenant who allows her dog to play in the hallway. Imagine opening your door and having a neighbor's dog run into your apartment, because, of course, he is not trained to "come" when called.

In order to not offend, schedule regular grooming appointments and teach your pet apartment manners.

APARTMENT BUILDING ELEVATORS

As a pet owner, you should also show consideration for your neighbors in apartment building elevators. While waiting for the elevator, your pet should "sit" quietly. Once in the elevators, either hold him or have him sit in the back left corner of the elevator next to the wall. I suggest positioning him in the back left corner because most riders look to the right before entering the elevator. Either way, if he is sitting in the elevator when the elevator door opens, potential passengers can decide if they want to enter and ride with you and your dog or wait for the next car. Also, by positioning your pet this way, you can turn and stand in front of him, and keep him calm and focused for the short ride up or down.

WHAT CITY-DWELLING DOGS NEED TO LEARN

Other than learning how to sit in an elevator, an apartment-dwelling dog should learn to be calm when he sees a neighbor, and how to "shake" for a doorman's treat. If necessary, call for a tutor—a professional dog trainer who understands the living conditions of city dogs. And for playtime—the best part of having a dog—consider appropriate places, such as your home, the dog park, or a doggy daycare center rather than the common hallway.

DOG INTERVIEWS FOR ADMITTANCE TO CONDOS, CO-OPS, AND OTHER RESIDENTIAL BUILDINGS

In many metropolitan cities, before moving into a dog-friendly building, the governing board will request to meet your dog. These dog interviews have worried potential tenants and real estate agents alike, causing them to lose sleep, pull out their hair, or even drop a few pounds out of concern for the potential loss of a great home or of the lucrative commission thereon. The best way to make a good impression is to not wait until the last minute to prepare your dog for the interview.

If you find out that the building you would like to live in requires a dog interview, call a dog trainer immediately. Have her review the basics so that at the board interview your dog will be able to sit, stay, and lie down. Your dog should also be able to have the board representative pet her without her getting too excited, jumping up, or baring her teeth. To really impress the interviewer, have the dog trainer teach your dog to shake the interviewer's hand.

While you are working with a trainer, you should be simultaneously creating a doggy dossier with supporting documentation to bring to the interview. This dossier should contain a canine resume describing your dog—his history, personality, health, training, and any other qualifications that will emphasize that he is a good boy and not a nuisance. In your one-page profile, include his name, breed, age, and weight. If his breeder is a top breeder of AKC Champion White West Highland terriers, who breeds for beauty, brains, and temperament, mention that your dog is the most exemplary of his breeding program. If your mixed-breed, who was born at the local shelter, visits nursing homes and children's hospitals on the weekends, highlight that he is dedicated to his work. If he doesn't have a desirable pedigree or a special job, but his main task in life is to keep you happy, then don't hesitate to mention that he is a loving companion and great family member.

Because many buildings have size and weight restrictions, always include two pictures of your pet. The first picture should be of his face and the second should be a full body profile. In your package, also include a certificate from your veterinarian attesting that your dog is in good health and up-to-date on all of her vaccinations. You may also want to list the name of your dog walker and assure the board that the walker is bonded and insured. In past years, this has proven to be very important, since there have been occurrences of biting incidents that have happened on building premises while the dog was in the care of a pet professional. If you have a certificate of accomplishment from a dog-training school, or a recommendation from your obedience

PET TIP

If you bring a dog home, tell your neighbors. Call them directly and tell them the good news. Don't just leave the message about your new pet. Wait and speak to them directly. Let them know that you are concerned that the dog might bark and disturb them until he gets settled in his new surroundings, and ask for their patience and understanding. Assure them that you are implementing a schedule so that the pooch will adjust as quickly as possible.

trainer attesting that your dog has learned basic skills and is able to sit in elevators and walk through the lobby nicely on lead, add it to the package.

BARKING BLUES

The biggest complaint of both suburbanites and city dwellers is a barking dog. Although dogs bark as a means of communication, barking becomes a real problem when it is deemed to be excessive. Some breeds, such as terriers (Yorkshire, Cairn, West Highland White), are genetically prone to bark more frequently. Other dogs that are improperly confined or lack socialization bark as a means of frustration, and dogs that get an insufficient amount of exercise bark as a way to burn off some energy. Environmental sounds such as other barking dogs, the ringing of a phone or doorbell, unfamiliar voices, and street sounds can excite barking; separation anxiety can also be a factor.

The problem with this excessive vocalization is that it can be a nuisance to your neighbors wherever you live. Before neighbors report you to the apartment building board, the regulating community body, or, even worse, the police, you need to take control of your dog and train him to stop barking.

SOLVING BAD BARKING

The key to solving a barking problem is to determine what is triggering the barking behavior. If you confine your dog, determine whether his shelter or crate is adequate. For a dog that is kept outside, provide him with a clean, comfortable, climate-controlled, and roomy shelter. Frankly, I believe that there is never a good reason for your dog to live outside or away from family life. For those people who want a dog for protection, realize that a dog can warn you of danger from the inside just as easily as he can from the outside of a home. For a dog that is crated indoors, make certain that the size of the kennel is appropriate for his size. Your dog should be able to stand up, turn around, and lie down comfortably in his crate. As he grows bigger, get a larger crate and make it comfortable with clean bedding. Dogs that are crated for long hours, without a regular schedule of bathroom breaks and playtime, can become big barkers.

Easing barking could be as easy as changing your dog's daily routine. Aside from a regular activity schedule, a good diet and exercise regime is very helpful in modifying a dog's behavior. Dogs should be fed a nutritious meal twice a day and should have access to fresh, clean water a few times a day.

Although you may have a yard or terrace in which he can play, you should take your dog for at least one walk each day around the neighborhood for physical and mental stimulation. Not only will he stay fit, but he will be able to spend time with you, enjoying your company. Moreover, if he is friendly toward other dogs, take him to the local dog run so that he can burn off some energy and socialize with other dogs. These daily routine activities, when kept up, can help ease barking.

Another good idea to curb barking is to purchase new toys, some that promote human and dog interaction so the two of you can play together and others that can keep him occupied while he is home alone. For example, a ball is great for good game of fetch, and a laser pointer is an entertaining way for him to keep in shape, chasing the point of light. When he is home alone, give him busy-box toys that dispense either toys or treats as he paws and nudges at them. This self-motivating play can help keep him calm and quiet. However, if your time is very limited, hire a daily dog walker who can spend quality time with him, participating in these activities.

If environmental sounds stimulate his barking, limit his access to them. While you are out, leave him in the quietest part of the house and away from the windows. Close the drapes, turn off the ringer on the phone, and leave on a radio or a television to drown out noise.

Sometimes changes in environment don't help and you need to teach him to be quiet on command. Don't expect to train him to stop barking overnight. It takes a while to integrate the command into his life.

MISS FIDO MANNERS ON . . .
Postal Workers and Delivery Persons

According to the U.S. Postal Service, since 2001 more than 3,000 postal employees have been bitten by dogs. To prevent the letter carrier from being bitten, keep your dog inside, away from the door, and preferably in another room; it is also ill advised to let your dog loose in your yard. Don't encourage your child to take mail from the carrier in the presence of your family dog, who could perceive that your child is in danger and attack. Although mailmen and other delivery persons are trained to deal with dogs and discouraged from petting them, you may ask your carrier to meet your dog to prevent him from barking, pacing, or simply going crazy when he hears or sees a delivery person approaching your home. If they agree, allow them to meet your leashed dog and have them give your pet a biscuit once he is calmly sitting. If your pet learns that these visitors look forward to seeing and rewarding him for his good behavior, he will learn to act politely upon their arrival. And most importantly, don't forget to thank your mail carrier or delivery person for their participation in your dog's training.

Teach your dog to stop barking with the "Quiet" command. The next time he starts to bark, after a few woofs, tell him to be "Quiet" and show him a treat. Most dogs will hush for a treat. When he is silent, tell him "Good boy." After a few seconds of no barking, give him the treat. Little by little, increase the time that you make him wait for the treat. If he continues to bark after you give him a treat, tell him "No!" in a very loud voice and tell him "Quiet" again. Always praise him for obeying your commands. Gradually, as he learns to stop barking for food, substitute the food for petting. In due course, stop the food and the petting—just use praise, which should be sufficient as a reward.

If your dog continues to have barking issues, you can invest in a citronella collar. A citronella collar releases a spray when the microphone in the collar senses barking. These collars are more humane than static collars, or shock collars, which should only be used as a last resort. If you fear that your dog suffers from separation anxiety, contact your veterinarian about medication and other remedies that you can use in conjunction with these barking strategies.

BE CORDIAL, DON'T IMPOSE

Another way to maintain good neighborly relations is to never impose on your neighbors or ask their children to take care of your dog. When you go on holiday, take a business trip, or have family emergency, hire a professional pet sitter or send your dog to a kennel. Remember, if your neighbor does a horrendous job of taking care of your dog, or something happens to your home, it will sour your relationship permanently.

Lastly, if your neighbor complains about your pet, control yourself and don't direct your anger toward her. Better that she speaks or writes to you directly, rather than alerting a board or the authorities of your pooch's possible misbehavior. Whatever form she chooses to contact you, respond in the same manner in a timely fashion. In your communication to her, thank her for contacting you directly, assure her that you will look into the problem and solve it if your dog is the culprit, and assure her that you will get back to her quite soon.

As a pet owner, always try to maintain a cordial relationship with your neighbors, because there is a chance that you will be living next to them for longer than the life of your dog.

PRODUCT RESOURCE GUIDE

If you are concerned about dog owners' rights and interested in breed-ban legislation, visit the Web sites of the American Dog Owner's Association, Inc. (*www.adoa.org*); the American

Kennel Club (*www.akc.org*); or the American Society for the Prevention of Cruelty to Animals (*www.aspca. org*).

Concerned about pet fencing? Visit *www.petsafe.net* and find a wireless fence to keep your pet enclosed in your yard. PetSafe also offers citronella collars that can help with barking issues.

Browse the Web site of the Association of Professional Animal Waste Specialist (*www.apaws.org*) to find a professional pooper scooper near you.

Contact the Association of Pet Dog Trainers (*www .apdt.com*), International Association of Canine Professionals (*www.dogpro.org*); or the National Association of Dog Obedience Instructors (*www.nadoi.org*) to find a dog trainer to help you and your pet refine your behavior.

Chapter 7

THE *Pawfect* PET GIFT

I am proud to be known to friends, family members, and other dog lovers as an excellent gift-giver, because I always buy presents suited to the person, or in many cases, the dog, for whom I am buying. When choosing a pet-related gift, you must do the same. Take into consideration the person or dog for whom you are buying the gift.

NOT THE PERFECT GIFT

No matter how often he tells you that he wants a dog, it is ill-advised to buy a dog as a gift for a friend or an adult family member. Especially during the Christmas holidays, many people are gifted with pets, and by February many of them are trying to find better homes for these unwanted four-legged purchases. The decision to purchase a dog should be that of the potential dog owner, who is looking for a ten- to fifteen-year relationship with a dog of his choice that he deems a good fit for his lifestyle.

A potential dog owner needs to be mentally, physically, and monetarily prepared for owning a pet. He has to adjust his schedule to feed, water, exercise, play, and train his pooch in a consistent manner. Other dog owner tasks include puppy- or dog-proofing the home, as well as paying for veterinary services, dog food, pet sitting or kennel care, regular grooming sessions, and a variety of other services and products for many years to come.

All in all, the best gift for a friend who wants a dog is to purchase a few books about dog breeds and canine care. This way, he can decide for himself when and if he is ready for a dog.

GOOD GIFTS FOR HUMANS

The ideal gift for a dog lover or pet professional who cares for your dog is something dog-related that you know she will enjoy. Dog show tickets, a subscription to a dog magazine, a picture frame decorated with a canine motif, pet jewelry, or other pet-themed items are great gifts that can really be appreciated. Unless you know her favorite breed, abstain from buying her breed-specific mugs, calendars, T-shirts, socks, or other clothing.

BEST PRESENTS FOR DOGS

The best gifts to purchase are not for the owner but for the pooches of friends, family, neighbors, and business associates. When buying gifts for dogs, it is best to purchase toys, treats, or gift certificates that their owners can spend on them.

If you have an eye for fashion—including pet fashion—remember, pet clothing is not one-size-fits-all, so buying clothing for someone's dog other than your own can be rather difficult. If you want to buy something really special, give the dog owner a gift certificate for her favorite boutique. In the fall and winter months, pet boutiques are filled with the newest pet fashions, and your gift certificate could treat the gifted dog with a trendy coat, chic carrier, or hip leash and collar. Grooming gift certificates always make good gifts, too, because dog owners like to have their pets looking and smelling great.

As much as dogs enjoy looking stylish, if you want to buy a gift that a dog can really enjoy, then consider a toy. Don't leave home without knowing the dog's age, breed, sex, size, and activity level. Young pups like soothing toys that they can cuddle with or toys that they can chew, so small, soft stuffed toys and puppy teethers or rope toys are appropriate items for them. Adolescent dogs tend to be more active and need toys that can stimulate them, especially when they are home alone. Busy-box toys that release treats or toys, tougher chew toys, and larger stuffed toys are great for them. Toys like balls, Frisbees, or any interactive toy that encourages human and pet bonding are fitting, too. Senior dogs lounge more, so a bed or blanket that they can relax on is suitable.

When choosing a canine gift, also bear in mind breed characteristics. Terriers like to chase; hounds like to hunt; golden and Labrador retrievers like to fetch; German shepherds like to herd. The toy should be size-appropriate, too. With the substantial toy selection at most pet stores, if you are perplexed about what to buy, ask the staff for help. And if a toy comes in six colors, bring home pink for girl dogs and blue for boy dogs, because the owner most likely will appreciate it.

PET TIP

Before buying a canine gift, ask about the pet store's return policy, just in case the owner needs to bring it back and select something else.

In addition to toys, treats make yummy gifts. All dogs can enjoy a basket of healthy treats made from fresh ingredients and no chemicals or preservatives. Many dogs have allergies or are overweight, so when you send the healthiest treats possible, the dog's owner will not have to worry about additional doggy pounds or a compromised allergy-specific diet.

Buying the perfect presents for dogs and dog lovers is great fun; just buy gifts that are suitable, enjoyable, and can be appreciated.

Mike and his boxer, Plato, are a prime example of meaningful gift-giving. When they relocated from New

York to West Hollywood, they didn't know anyone. They soon became friends with Brian, their next-door neighbor, who was an artist. Although he was a dog lover, Brian didn't have a dog and, after gaining Mike's permission, he enjoyed taking walks with Plato while Mike was at work. Each day, Brian would walk Plato to a nearby pet store for a treat and then home again. One day, Plato preferred a toy to a treat, so Brian bought him the toy instead. It soon became Plato's favorite. He took it everywhere with him, and sometimes he even slept with it. After Plato died, Brian painted a picture of him with the favorite toy and gave it to Mike. Mike was so happy to receive it, he hung it up immediately. Brian died a few years ago, and Mike told me that every time he looks at that painting he thinks of them on their daily walk to the pet store.

PRODUCT RESOURCE GUIDE

To help with the process of finding a dog, buy *The Right Dog for You* by Daniel F. Tortora, Ph.D. (Fireside, 1983) at your favorite pet store or *www.amazon.com*.

For dog lovers, you can buy a gift subscription to *Dog Fancy Magazine* at *www.dogchannel.com*.

Another great gift for the purebred-dog enthusiast is the yearly poster of the Westminster Kennel Club Dog Show. The poster proceeds benefit the organization's therapy dog program, Angel on a Leash. See *www.westminsterkennelclub.org*.

Pet Stages creates developmental toys for the stages of a dog's life. Visit *www.petstages.com* to find a toy for a puppy, adult, or senior dog.

While Foppers Gourmet Pet Bakery makes beautifully decorated 100 percent natural treats with yogurt (*www.foppers.com*), Honeybark Bakery makes organic treats with whole grains, fruits, vegetables, fresh meats, nuts, seeds, and spices. There's something for every dog's taste here (*www.honeybark .com*).

Chapter 8

Proper PET *Party* PLANNING

Many pet parents want their canine kids to celebrate important dates, such as birthdays, in style with family, neighbors, and other four-legged friends. Pet parties are a fairly new and exciting idea for devoted owners—and dogs do love the company of other dogs! Getting a jump on the preparations will go a long way toward heading off the problems that can ruin any good party: unruly guests, a shortage of refreshments, or property destruction. Everyone's been to a party where the human guests acted like crazed animals. Taking care when planning a pet party ensures that the guests at your soiree will be perfectly civilized animals.

LOCATION AND GUEST LIST

When throwing a bow-wow bash, first recognize that canine guests need a sufficient amount of space and supervision, so go for either a backyard party or a catered affair at a doggy daycare or training center.

Package deals at such facilities include play space and staff assistance for an agreed-upon number of hours, and the personnel can also help you set up, monitor canine interaction, and expedite cleanup (but remember, all those hours will be reflected on your bill).

Once the location is booked, the next step is to consider the guest list. Professional party planners for people advise that you choose the guests wisely. They say that the key element to a successful event is to invite a stimulating group of people who represent a mix of interests. At canine events, the mix is just as important. In the interest of safety, it should also be limited to dogs with compatible personalities and good manners. Dogs that are already familiar with each other from the dog run, neighborhood, or doggy daycare center will be the most likely to play politely. Inviting guests who happen to be your friends with pets—rather than inviting your dog's friends and owners—is essentially inviting trouble.

INVITATIONS

Every good host knows that the invitation sets the tone for the party. Consider purchasing breed stationery to match that of your guest of honor, or buy festive, fill-in birthday invitations by the box at the local drug store. For a truly special invitation, have a pet photographer take a special picture of you and your pet. Beautiful photos are works of art, and the invitations will make great keepsakes for you and your guests. Remember to include the date, time, location, RSVP information, and the words "All canine guests must be accompanied by their owners." If you and the other pet owners tend to have very busy social lives, invitations should be sent out at least three weeks before the day of the party.

WHAT TO DO AND WHAT TO EAT

If you are the kind of host who loves to create an unforgettable event, consider hiring an obedience instructor who can teach party guests, old and new, some tricks. Agility exercises are an especially fun idea. Watching Jack, the Great Pyrenees, jump over planks and barrel through tunnels is just as much fun as watching Natalie, the long-haired Chihuahua, discover her athletic ability on a low hurdle.

After deciding on the location, service, and entertainment for your fete, consider the menu. Dogs might enjoy a birthday cake from the famous Three Dog Bakery. If you prefer baking yourself, liver cupcakes topped with cream cheese and peanut butter icing are a big hit with the kibble crowd. With the menu planned, don't forget the beverage of choice at these dogged affairs is cool, fresh water served in multiple dog bowls—and with these guests, plenty of it!

Have plenty of plastic bags on hand for poop-scooping, and, if the party is indoors, make sure there are rolls of paper towels and spray cleaner as well. Your human guests should clean up immediately after their own dogs, but if they don't, it's your job as host to make sure any mess is magically whisked away.

Each human guest should also be responsible for the safety of her own dog, but again, the hostess with the mostess will look out for all her partygoers. You wouldn't let a friend drive home drunk from a New Year's Eve bash at your house; likewise, you shouldn't let any dog at your party do anything you know to be dangerous.

MISS FIDO MANNERS ON . . .
Pet Parties

One of the highlights of going to doggy soirees is to see what costumes the other dogs are wearing. If you are going to dress your dog in a costume, purchase a pet costume from your local pet store or a doggy boutique. Never buy a child's costume and try to modify for your pet, because it could be uncomfortable as well as a hazard. And don't expect to just stand around with your dog—take part in the games and other activities. You'll have so much fun that you'll soon be making plans for your own!

At a Halloween party I once threw, one of my guests had bought a child's giraffe costume for his dog, and then modified it by pinning the cloth with safety pins to fit the dog's body. Not only was there the possibility that one of the pins could open and stick the dog, the modified costume turned out to be a choking hazard too. I saw the dog almost choke as the costume slipped down and pulled at his neck. I went directly to the poor pooch and unpinned the cloth, then said to my guest as sweetly as I could, "I guess Jonas will just come as himself today; I don't want to see him uncomfortable."

THEME-SPECIFIC PARTY IDEAS

If you can't wait for the next pet party invitation, throw a party for your dog. Use some of the ideas below as a starting point.

Halloween: These parties are my absolute favorite and the most popular parties I give. For the last few years, I have hosted a Halloween party with my four dogs. I spend at least three days decorating a room at a doggy daycare center with a team of young designers who love to help me make the place look like a haunted house with dilapidated furniture, portraits of doggy ancestors, cobwebs, and scary music. Each year, I invite the same twenty to twenty-five canine guests and their owners. The highlight is the doggy costumes, because they get better and better each year. The invitees are extremely competitive and try to outdo each other every year. My favorites are a Yorkshire terrier dressed as Sherlock Holmes and a mixed breed disguised as King Kong with Deluxe Tower attached. Dogs and their owners love the trick-y games, such as bobbing for apples, the pumpkin and apple cupcakes with cream cheese frosting, and, of course, my treat bags full of great books, fun toys, and tasty snacks.

Bark Mitzvah: While some religious leaders and others deem these coming-of-age celebrations as unorthodox, some individuals view them all in good fun and prefer to have these parties during Purim, a time of merrymaking, carnival, and parodies. These types of parties are not for me, but I understand the need of a dog owner to share his life with his dog, even if that means his spiritual lifestyle. That is why kosher dog food and treats exist, as well as Jewish toys for dogs. See *www. kosherpets.com* and *www.oytoys.com.*

Bow Vows: In 2006, Pamela Anderson held a wedding for her golden retriever and her Chihuahua on the beach in Malibu. I don't think it is necessary for dogs to marry, because, frankly, they have other mating rituals that are best served without throwing a wedding party for them. Better yet, invite your dog to be a wedding guest or participant in your own wedding, like Adam Sandler did with his English bulldog, Meatball, or Gwen Stefani and her husband, Gavin Rossdale, did with their Puli, Winston. To find doggy wedding attire, search Groom Doggy at *www.groomdoggy.com*.

Holiday Party: Have an evening affair to remember! Invite canine guests to dress in tuxedos, gowns, or cocktail dresses, which can be bought at pet stores or pet boutiques. Prior to the party, organize a Secret Santa so that guests can exchange gifts. Serve holiday-themed cookies on silver trays (*www.foppers.com*).

Bow-Wow Luau: These beach-themed parties don't have to take place at the seashore, but can be held at a dog park or in your backyard. Just buy baby pools and fill them with water to create the seaside ambience. Guest dogs can wear bathing suits, Hawaiian print shirts, grass skirts, or dress au natural. Serve mini-hamburgers, hot dogs, and doggy ice cream as a special dessert (*www.dogateers. com*). Dogs can play on the sand or swim in the water for entertainment. Hire a dog trainer to teach dogs tricks.

Mardi Gras: For dog owners who like to have outrageous parties with their dogs, celebrate Mardi Gras. Dogs can come as fairies, jesters, or clowns, or kings or other members of the royal court; they can wear feather boas (*www.hmb-seattle.com*) or come to the party painted in colors of gold, green, and purple. Better to have your groomer color your dog with food coloring than make a mess in your home. Create a memorable parade by decorating Radio Flyer wagons (*www.radioflyer.com*) as floats. Smaller dogs can ride on the floats and the larger can march in a parade—all to Zydeco music. Serve traditional food such as King cake, a round, yellow cake with a yogurt glaze of three, special colors.

Pajama Party: Remember when you got together with a group of friends and spent the night together eating, drinking, listening to music, and watching movies? Today, pajama parties for dogs and their owners are held in fashionable hotels. Those who are spending a night in the hotel congregate in a host's suite for snacks, and flicks like *Must Love Dogs, You've Got Mail, Lady and the Tramp*, and *The Truth about Cats and Dogs*. Dogs and their owners can wear matching pajamas (*www.gidget gear.com*) and get massages before bedtime. The Ritz-Carlton in Sarasota, Florida, offers in-room pet massage therapy (*www.ritzcarlton.com*).

Spa Day: Promote doggy health and wellness. Turn your backyard into a wellness garden, or a room in your home into a health spa. Hire holistic professionals to provide the entertainment. An aromatherapist can use scented oils to restore pet senses and spirits; a dog masseuse can help canine guests relax; and a dog groomer can clip nails and trim up coats. Dogs should wear spa robes (*www.animalwrappers.com*), drink bottled water (*www.doggiesprings.com*), and feast on health biscuits. Play Dog Dreams: Relaxing Music for Dogs, and Dog Lovers (*www.petslovemusic.com*).

Tailwag: If your dog is athletic and likes to play ruff with his friends, have a tailwag party. Dogs can wear football, baseball, and soccer jerseys with matching team leads (*www.huntermfg.com, www.sportyk9.com, www.doggystyledesigns.com*). Hire a dog trainer, who can teach agility and organize competitive team games with owners and their dogs. Dogs will love the full menu of doggy brew (*www.doggiebrew.com*) and homemade chili—minus the onions and the spices—served over rice.

Mad Hatters Party: Call up some of your girlfriends and organize an afternoon garden party. Dogs and their owners can dress up and enjoy their time together outdoors. Female dogs can wear pretty party dresses (*www.barkingbaby.com*) and male dogs can wear formal T-shirts (*www.iseespot.com*), or you

PET TIP

Don't let your party go entirely to the dogs! Remember to serve refreshments for the owners. Serve water, juice, and soda for the owners in paper cups only, since glass containers could shatter and injure party guests. Also, avoid hot drinks that could spill and scald. Serving snacks to the owners could be difficult, because dogs might whine and beg for food, so use your discretion.

can dress your dogs in costumes such as a bumblebee or ladybug, with angel wings (*www.groomdoggy.com*), delicate bows (*www.hmb-seattle.com*), exquisite jewelry, and beautiful leashes and collars. But all pets and their owners must wear fun and outrageous toppers. Serve a light lunch of chicken over rice with vegetables. The idea of this party is for your dog to be seen, to be social, and to be impressive.

Wild West Woof Down: If you love to play cowboys and Indians, have a Wild West party. Dogs can come dressed in cowboy or cowgirl outfits, ponchos and sombreros, and even cow costumes. Take pictures of dogs in their costumes, and create Wanted posters by using Photoshop or a similar computer program. To make things fun, hire a freestyle instructor (*www.worldcaninefreestyle.org*) to teach the dogs and their owners how to square dance. Serve Cowboy Cookout, Venison Stew, Wild Buffalo Grill, or Wildness Blend (*www.merrickpetcare.com*).

Once the party is over, send your guests off in style with doggy bags. Don't forget that even after the lights are out and the party's over, a pet parent must complete all of the responsibilities of a good host. Write thank-you notes to those guests who brought your pet a present.

Pet parties offer a unique opportunity to promote social interaction between dogs and their owners. While at these events, take advantage of the planned activities.

Games and training activities allow you to utilize your special relationship and to work together as the team that you are.

PRODUCT RESOURCE GUIDE

For truly memorable pet portraits, consider photographer Jim Dratfield. Although he lives in New York City, he will travel throughout the world for clients. Reach him at *www.petography.com*.

For party planners on a budget who still want to have dog-training fun, try *My Dog Can Do That!* a board game of seventy-two training tricks, for about $21 from *www.SitStay.com*.

You'll find Three Dog Bakery at *www.threedog.com*. The peanut butter cake is very popular and can be shipped throughout the United States. Order it a week in advance to ensure you will have it for the party.

Great recipes for other canine cooking can be found in the *Three Dog Bakery Cookbook,* by Dan Dye and Mark Beckloff (Andrews McMeel, 1998) and *Doggy Desserts: Homemade Treats for Happy, Healthy Dogs* by Cheryl Gianfrancesco (BowTie Press, 2007).

Chapter 9

FOUR-LEGGED
Wedding GUESTS

Tradition dictates that the bride and groom celebrate their wedding nuptials with as many family members as possible. If your family includes both the two- and four-legged varieties, why wouldn't you want to share your special day with your dog and have her join the party?

If your Pomeranian is a barker, your mixed breed is a jumper, or your giant schnauzer is not used to being around people, think twice about having your dog attend the wedding or incorporating her into the ceremony. Dealing with a dog that has a behavior problem or erratic behavior will only increase the stress of a day that you want to be perfect. But if your dog is a good girl who can easily adapt to the excitement of a special occasion, you should share your special day with her. She can play a role, such as flower girl or bridesmaid, or be simply a guest at your nuptials.

OBTAINING PERMISSION FROM OFFICIANT AND VENUE

The idea of having your dog participate in the wedding festivities is exciting, but you will need to plan ahead. Before determining her supporting role, you will need to have permission from the venue. If you are getting married in a house of worship, discuss the idea with your priest, minister, pastor, or rabbi. If the officiant seems a bit surprised by your request, explain to him that your pet is an important family member. You can remind him that many houses of worship are involved in pet-related activities, such as the Blessing of the Animals, a yearly event held at some houses of worship to bless family pets. It will help to clarify how she will be incorporated into your ceremony, and assure the venue representative that she will be chaperoned throughout the ceremony, and removed immediately if she displays any distracting behavior. If you prefer to get married on a local beach, at a park, or in a garden, don't be surprised if those venue representatives deny your request to have her participate. Many municipalities do not allow dogs on the beach during the summer months, nor are dogs allowed in certain park or garden areas reserved for special events. Some indoor venues, like a wedding center or a hotel, might approve her presence at the ceremony, but be prepared to pay a pet fee.

If you do obtain permission, next discuss the idea with your wedding party. It is important that wedding party members feel comfortable around your dog, and that you make provisions for those who are allergic to pets. Once you receive feedback from your bridesmaids, grooms-men, and parents, you will have a better idea of how to incorporate her into your big day.

PREPARING POOCH FOR THE CEREMONY

Just as you and your betrothed take dance lessons to achieve the desired results, hire a dog trainer to teach your dog how to behave for the occasion. Your trainer should review walking nicely on a leash, so that she can walk down the aisle with ease; sitting, so she can sit still for photographs; and standing, so she can stand in place in the receiving line. Also, if you are fond enough of your dog trainer, ask if he could serve as your pooch's escort on your wedding day. By doing so, you will not have to be involved in transporting your dog to and from your home, house of worship, or reception. Also, as your dog's escort, your trainer can be responsible for walking, feeding, and supervising your dog with other guests—giving you one less thing to worry about.

Hiring a pet coordinator paid off for Josie, a bride who was neither exceptionally fond of dogs nor of her soon-to-be mother-in-law. When her mother-in-law announced that she was bringing her dog to the wedding, Josie feared that her future in-law would drink too much and lose sight of her Toy poodle. When she told her wedding planner about the dog, the wedding planner told her not to worry; they would hire a pet coordinator, whose duties would include making sure the pet's needs were met. The pet coordinator did such a good job taking care of the pet and the mother-in-law that Josie didn't think twice about either of them, allowing her to really enjoy her special day.

WEDDING BEAUTY AND APPAREL

Also, don't wait until the last minute to take care of your dog's beauty needs. To have her looking beautiful, befitting such an important occasion, schedule a dog-grooming appointment weeks in advance. As a special request, ask the groomer to make sure that he thoroughly brushes your dog to remove all shedding hair from her coat and that he treats her with an anti-allergen product. This will ensure that allergy sufferers will be comfortable on your wedding day. And, if you want her dressed to impress, select apparel or accessories that she will feel comfortable wearing. Many brides and grooms prefer that their dog dress similarly to the bridal party, with their female dogs wearing gowns or their male dogs dressed in tuxedos, all of which are available at fine pet retailers. Another, more expensive option is to hire a seamstress to design a doggy gown or appropriate cummerbund in the bridal party colors. If you prefer not to dress a dog up, chose a special bandana, bow tie, or matching collar and lead set to create an elegant look. Whatever clothing or accessorizing options you choose, have your dog wear the outfit a few times before the event to get used to the feel of it.

FINAL CONSIDERATIONS FOR WEDDING INVOLVEMENT

Never underestimate the need for your dog to participate in the wedding rehearsal the day before. Although she may have been coached on how to act, don't make the mistake of introducing your dog to the venue on the day of the wedding. Take the time to familiarize your dog with the location more than once. On the big day, nothing could be worse than her greeting all the guests in their pews or having her creeping down the aisle in fear or eliminating on the carpet, causing a cleanup delay. Even though it may be amusing to some, it's not a favorable start to a special day.

PET TIP

If you are working with a wedding planner, discuss how you would like to incorporate your dog into your wedding day at your initial consultation. She most likely will have a list of venues that will allow dogs and some great ideas as well.

If your dog is playing the role of flower girl or ring bearer, there are some specific considerations to keep in mind. Some flowers and plants are poisonous if ingested by pets, and wedding flower arrangements and bouquets are often constructed with wire that could injure pets if not properly applied to a collar. Instead, you could have her wear a flower motif collar and lead. For a dog serving as a ring bearer, make sure your pooch is comfortable with either carrying the ring pillow, which attaches to his neck, or wearing ring "wings" on his back. Double-check to see that accessories have been applied correctly so as to prevent a choking hazard. Moreover, he still has to allow the best man to take the jewelry from him; this, too, will require a few practice sessions.

Lastly, note that, because of most local health codes, restaurants and banquet halls will not permit canine guests inside dining areas. However, if your reception is at home, your dog handler can supervise the mealtime activity. Remind the handler that under no circumstances should human guests treat your dog to human food. An emergency trip to the vet isn't desirable on such an auspicious day. Just in case, provide the handler with your veterinarian's telephone number and your credit card information. You could even arrange for the trainer to whisk your dog off to a few days at camp (at a kennel) directly after the ceremony, leaving you one less thing to think about afterwards or during your honeymoon.

PRODUCT RESOURCE GUIDE

For a refresher course in doggy wedding manners, browse the Association of Pet Dog Trainers (*www.apdt.com*), International Association of Canine Professionals (*www.dogpro.org*), and the National Association of Dog Obedience Instructors (*www.nadoi.org*) Web sites to find a dog trainer near you.

To reduce the allergic reactions of your wedding party and guests to your dog, treat your pet with Allerpet to cleanse the hair of dander, saliva, and sebaceous-gland secretions (*www.allerpet.com*).

To find doggy wedding attire, search Groom Doggy at *www.groomdoggy.com* or *www.iseespot.com*. For flower dogs, Canini Pet (*www.caninipet.com*) offers floral motif collar and leash sets made from leather.

For a list of dangerous plants and flowers, review the Humane Society of the United States Web site at *www.hsus.org*.

PART III

Etiquette Out and About

Chapter 10

STREET *Smarts*

Walking your dog is a necessary activity that gives him the opportunity to eliminate, exercise, and spend time bonding with you. But while you are out and about, remember that your behavior can affect those around you. As leader of your canine team, abide by the municipal rules, think before you act, and behave courteously, and you can successfully deal with chance encounters or any other circumstances with which you are confronted while out on the streets.

Most cities have dog license, leash, and canine waste ("pooper scooper") laws. Telephone your city Health Department's Office of Veterinary Affairs to inquire as to where you can find the pet laws pertaining to dog ownership. All in all, a good dog and his owner are a team and should always follow local rules and regulations regarding pets. You should have your dog wear rabies, license, and identification tags; keep him on a leash in public; pick up waste; and not create any nuisances with your pet. Once you understand these pet regulations, obey them.

COMMON PET REGULATIONS

License laws: Licensing is an important element in animal control and the protection of public health. Compiled information about licensed dogs assists in the medical follow-up of persons who were potentially exposed to rabies-infected or other seriously ill dogs. Licensing also helps to reunite lost dogs with their owners and enforces the state spay/neuter laws.

Leash laws: These laws reduce the possibility that dogs will annoy, attack, or bite people and/or other dogs, as well as lessen the likelihood that dogs will leave canine waste on the streets, in parks, or on lawns.

Canine waste or pooper scooper laws: Picking up your dog's waste reduces the spread of disease that can be transferred to people and other pets.

Rabies laws: Most city codes require that all animal bites be reported to the municipality's health department. The animal bite unit receives those reports and coordinates follow-up with the animal, the owner, and the person bitten to ensure that no further threat exists. This is important because rabies is a disease that can be fatal in humans. The law requires that all owned dogs be vaccinated against rabies.

MISS FIDO MANNERS ON . . .
Local Transportation

While most service dogs are allowed by law on subways and buses, in cabs, and on trains, check with your local department of transportation to find out specific pet regulations. In most cases, animals that are not properly or adequately secured in a kennel or carrier will be refused admittance on trains, buses, and subways and in taxis. In most metropolitan cities, a taxi driver will pick you up with your animal, not necessarily during rush hour, if your dog appears composed and clean. But if he is a little rough around the edges and in need of a pet etiquette class, coax him into a state of docility with a tasty snack. Have him "Sit–Stay" on the corner until a cab driver offers to transport you. Once you arrive at your destination, give a larger than normal tip to thank the driver for picking you up (and encourage him to transport other dogs and their owners). Lastly, if your dog sits on the seat next to you, rather than on the floor, be considerate of the next passenger and wipe down the seat before you exit the car.

WALKING AS EXERCISE

Although a regular walking regimen is the primary exercise, when deciding how far to walk, remember to take into consideration a dog's age, breed, and size, as well as the weather conditions. Although puppies have a lot of energy and are still learning to walk on a leash, take them for short walks until they master walking on a lead. The great outdoors provides stimulation for senior pets; just walk slowly and keep the distance short. In hot weather, flat-faced dogs, like Pugs, might have trouble breathing so keep their outdoor activity to a minimum.

LEASH IT ALL IN

A leash and collar are essential equipment to control your dog. When taking your dog for a walk, use a six-foot lead. Only use the retractable lead for the park, where your dog has open space to walk far ahead. When walking multiple dogs, use the same size leads for better control. A six-foot lead is perfect for walking in the neighborhood or on the city streets, and when the sidewalk is full of pedestrians, you can easily use it to rein him in, allowing him to walk in a heel position, close to you. Otherwise, give him the slack to walk comfortably, sniff, and do his business.

DOGGY BUSINESS

When your dog has to eliminate, teach him to eliminate by the curb. The phrase or signs that read "Curb Your Dog" mean that dog owners should have their dogs eliminate near the curbs or on the street and never in adjacent grass or in a tree pit. The purpose of curbing your dog is twofold. The first is to keep the sidewalks clean and the second is to facilitate picking up your dog's waste. It is much easier to clean up after your pooch curbside than it is in the middle of a busy sidewalk, where you can hinder the flow of traffic. Also, should you not be able to clean up all of the poop, you never have to worry that someone will step in it.

While in the city, dispose of all waste in the corner garbage can. If you are in the suburbs, there usually aren't any cans on the corners, so you might have to carry it home and deposit it in your own trash. Putting it in a neighbor's garbage can is an unwelcome surprise and simply rude.

DON'T LEAVE HOME WITHOUT THE EQUIPMENT

To avoid most poop problems, be sure to have plenty of poop bags. Even so, there may be an occasion when you either have forgotten the baggies or don't have enough. Don't get nervous and don't be shy. Politely ask a pedestrian if he has a tissue or newspaper that you can use, or solicit another dog owner for a poop bag. If there is no one who can help you, look for something on the street that you can use. If you live in a larger metropolitan city, you can walk over to the nearest corner and, as a last resort, use one of the free community newspapers or circulars that are placed in a display rack.

It is usually the case that when you walk away from a pile of poop, a screaming stranger will come out of nowhere demanding that you clean up your dog's waste. Although your first reaction might be to tell the poop patrol to be quiet, remember, this person doesn't realize that you have every intention to scoop. Politely explain that you ran out of bags and ask if she can help you by providing you with a bag, newspaper, or something that you can use to clean up after your dog. By asking for her assistance, you might actually get lucky and calm her down. More importantly, remember to pay it forward. Always help those in need by offering a baggie, because you never know when you will need one yourself.

This was once the case for Sophie when she decided to walk with her dogs to Staples to pick up some office supplies. A few minutes after she left the house, she met her neighbors. Her neighbor's son, Alex, a vivacious young man, loves her dogs so much that Sophie always enjoys being around him. With his mother's permission, Alex accompanied Sophie and the dogs to the store. As they walked to the store, her older Cavalier King Charles

Spaniel pooped for the second time. Sophie didn't have another bag, so she told Alex that she would pick up the poop on their return trip from the store, because she knew that she could ask the cashier for a plastic bag. Within seconds, Alex saw another dog owner across the street, ran over to him, and asked if they could "borrow" a poop bag. The other dog owner agreed, and Alex ran back across the street with the bag so the waste could be cleaned up. Alex, an eleven-year-old, taught Sophie a valuable lesson that day: ask and it shall be given.

CELL PHONES AS DISTRACTIONS

Once you know the community rules, have a handle on the proper equipment, and understand the nuances of poop protocol, you will need to master the art of walking with poochie. The task is to focus on where you are going and what your dog is doing. This can be difficult, especially if you are chatting on your cell phone. Of course you can do both, but if you do there is a greater chance that (a) you will miss the traffic light change, (b) your dog will woof down some gutter gourmet delicacy, or (c) you will bump into another pedestrian or his dog. The health and safety of you and your pet should always be your first concern, so, when walking your dog, stay off the phone and pay him some attention.

WALKING AND TALKING TO STRANGERS

While walking, anticipate interruptions. If you have a puppy, an unusual looking pooch, or a dog that oozes personality, expect that pet lovers will want to stop you so that they can pet and play with your dog. Use your best judgment when allowing someone to touch your dog. Nicely explain to your dog's fans that he must be sitting before he can receive a pet. Have your dog sit at your side and then allow the animal lover to pet him. If you do not have time to stop and engage the pet lover, smile and politely explain that your dog is in train-

PET TIP

If you are walking for a longer time or greater distance than normal, always bring along some water to quench your pet's thirst.

ing. Then you and your dog can move on quickly. Never be rude. You should be flattered, because it just goes to show you that others see just how special your dog is.

If by chance you meet a dog lover who wants to "treat" your pet with more than a pet, but with a dog biscuit, proceed with caution. I do not allow my dogs to take cookies from strangers. If you feel uncomfortable, thank them and tell them "My dog has a very strict diet" or "He is not allowed to eat between meals." Or to avoid conflict, take the biscuit and tell the giver you will save it for later.

97

CHANCE DOGGY MEET-AND-GREETS

With so many people owning dogs these days, it is almost impossible to walk down the street and not meet another dog and his owner. Before allowing dogs to greet each other, ask the owner if his dog is friendly and whether his dog can meet yours. Before a meet-and-greet, allow the other dog owner to make the decision. If he says, "No, not today," don't be rude—just move on. If he agrees, allow the dogs to interact for a few minutes. If the dogs seem to be playing too aggressively, growling, or jumping all over, or if the hair on the neck of one of them rises, pull your dog away and say "Thank you," and "Good-bye," and move on, as these are telltale signs to part ways.

Although some dogs are sweet as sugar, and others are a bit spicy or a tad temperamental, there are some that are just plain sour or nasty every time you see them. One of these personalities might even describe your dog. So if you see an aggressive dog coming toward you or your dog, acting as if he is spoiling for a fight—like many terriers do, for instance—don't panic, because your dog will feel your emotion as you tense up on the leash. Put your dog in the heel position and continue on your way. As you approach the other dog, command your dog, "Let's go," all while picking up the pace. Whatever you do, don't make matters worse by stopping or acknowledging the other dog and his owner. This will encourage either your dog or the other dog to behave more belligerently. Once you have adequate distance between you and the other dog and his owner, slow your pace down.

MISS FIDO MANNERS ON . . .
Pet Shuttles

If public transportation is not for you, another option is to arrange for a pet transportation company to service your needs. These shuttle vans are climate-controlled and designed so that you and your dog can arrive at your destination comfortably and sans stress. Dogs can ride either confined to a crate in the back or next to you, as long as they are secured with a safety belt or in a car seat, which the service provides. "Pet taxis" can drive you and your dog to the veterinarian, groomer, or boarding kennel. They will even take you on a longer trip, driving you a few hours or through a few states until you reach your selected destination. Prices vary, based on time of day and length of trip. Before sitting in the passenger seat with your pooch, get recommendations and confirm that the service is licensed and insured. And, as with any cab or car service, don't hesitate to tip the driver for a nice trip!

CORNER CROSSINGS

As you continue your dog walk, it is a good idea to cross at the corners to prevent a serious mishap. Too many accidents have occurred because individuals with their dogs have darted out from between parked cars. When at the corner, and if the weather is good (because I rather my dogs not sit and get themselves dirtier or wetter on a rainy or snowy day), have your dog sit at least two feet away from the curb. When you position yourself in this spot, pedestrians can see you and your dog from all sides and decide whether they want to stand near you. While waiting for the light, don't let your dog nuzzle strangers or stick his nose in baby strollers. A wet nose is not pleasurable for everyone, and some pedestrians might be offended by your dog's presumptuous behavior.

Lastly, and what I discourage most, is running a quick errand with your dog unless you know that you can bring him into the store with you. It is bad manners to tie your dog up to a parking meter or other outdoor post for a number of reasons. Besides deterring drivers from parking in certain spots, motorists will be afraid to approach your dog to put coin in the meter or will fear that your dog will jump up on their car and scratch it. It is likewise dangerous to leave your dog tied up outside because he might be stolen or deter other patrons from visiting the store.

While out on the street with your dog, your behavior can affect motorists, pedestrians, and dogs and their owners. Behaving courteously will ensure a more enjoyable time while out and about on the town.

PRODUCT RESOURCE GUIDE

Take care of business and the environment with Spike Brand Business Bags. Made from corn, these biodegradable bags will disintegrate within forty-five days (*www.spikebrand.com*).

If your dog is a messy poopster, try Poop-Freeze, a specially formulated aerosol freeze spray that hardens dog poop for easier pickup. The product is non-flammable, contains no CFCs, and is perfect for indoor and outdoor use (*www.poopfreeze.com*).

Coastal makes leashes and collars in a variety of sizes and lengths. Find one for your dog at *www.coastalpet .com*. For a retractable lead for the park, visit *www.flexi usa.com*.

Because our dogs don't wear shoes, we need to protect their feet during extreme weather conditions. Musher's Secret paw protector will keep salt from affecting his pads in the snow and protect them from the hot asphalt in warm temperatures. To find, visit your local pet store.

If you need a little more control walking your dog, try a martingale style collar (a type of collar that a dog wears comfortably loose and that tightens only when it needs to be tight for gentle control) or a Gentle Leader™ head halter (a halter designed to make if difficult for dogs to pull by causing a dog's nose to be turned down and back toward the owner). See *www.premier.com.*

Chapter 11

Best Practices AT THE DOG RUN

If you would like your four-legged kid to interact, socialize, and play with other dogs, I suggest that you visit the neighborhood dog park. Depending on where you live and what term you prefer, the "dog park" or "dog run" is the melting pot of modern dogdom. It truly represents the interaction of all breeds and canine mixes, with their diverse dog owners using an outdoor location as a friendly, sociable gathering place. It is the playful epicenter of all things dog-related in a community.

DIFFERENT TYPES OF DOG PARKS

There are many types of dog parks, with various rules and regulations. Some are public while others are private, membership-only locations. Some also have separate spaces for big and small dogs. There are dog parks with enclosed or open spaces and areas where you can spend time with your dog in an on-leash or off-leash doggy play area. No matter what kind of dog park is available, you and your dog have the opportunity to meet new friends in your community. One way to locate your local dog park is to visit your resident parks department Web site and look for a listing of dog runs in your town. And, please, become familiar with both the written rules and the unwritten customs of the dog run.

In most communities, dogs that are licensed by the local municipality may use the dog park. Prior to entering the play area, all dogs must be properly inoculated and parasite-free, and their owners must clean up after their pets and pay close attention to their actions. Your dog should wear a basic flat buckle collar containing her city license, rabies, and other identification. Pinch and spike collars are generally not allowed to prevent dogs from injuring themselves.

Seem simple enough? Not necessarily. The world of dog runs can also be a vicious social circle. Make sure you and your dog are always on your best behavior and mind your doggy manners.

SOCIAL MANNERS AT THE PARK

Come to the dog park appropriately dressed by wearing clothes that can be soiled and shoes that are comfortable. Nothing is worse than wearing a new outfit only to have it ruined by muddied paws or poop from a slip-

and-fall in high heels. You will be much better received if you come with a friendly and playful dog. Never bring an aggressive dog into the run for fear of her bullying or hurting other dogs. If you do, it is likely that the other dog owners will tell you to take your wild dog home.

In general, always be pleasant and considerate to the other pet parents. It is unsanitary and inappropriate to eat or drink at the dog park. Not only could the smell of food excite the dogs, but drinks and food could spill and be ingested by pets, causing them to be sick. Also, hot drinks could tumble over, burning you, your dog, and others.

Although you should not drink at the run, your dog may need to quench her thirst. As a preventive health measure, don't allow her to drink out of the park communal bowl. Take her aside, away from the other dogs, and give her water to drink from her own water bottle or bowl. If another dog owner asks if her dog can have a drink from your water bottle or bowl, politely refuse or offer to give them water by having her dog drink from a cup that she can find. If you are worried about upsetting another dog owner, give your dog water before you enter the dog run or after you exit the dog run.

GOSSIP AND LOVE FOUND

While socializing with the other dog owners, be cautious about discussing the particulars of your personal life or gossiping about fellow dog owners around you. Never brag about your dog's pedigree or good looks for fear of being labeled a dog snob. Should you or your dog find romance at the doggy playground, agree with your new mate to keep your relationship to yourselves, because you will be dog food for thought with the park regulars.

PET TIP

Always pay attention to your dog at the dog park. Owners need to watch for signs of doggy aggression. Teach your dog to come when called. If you spot trouble, call your dog to get her attention, as this helps to avoid fights.

While at the dog park, I once saw a young woman who spent so much time flirting with a handsome owner of a Bernese mountain dog that she didn't notice that her Petit Basset Griffon Vendéen had left the dog park. After a thorough search of the neighborhood (and the terrific-looking guy with the great smile did not help her), she came home to find the dog sitting in the lobby with her doorman. Lesson to be learned: treat your dog well; she will always be at home waiting for you. And don't let handsome or pretty dog owners distract you from taking care of your most faithful of companions, your dog.

PLAYING ROUGH

While at the dog run, keep all games on an even playing field, and encourage your dog to play according to her natural instincts—let her run, wrestle, and chase her playmates, but monitor her behavior closely to make sure she is playing appropriately with the other dogs. Never bring toys or treats to the dog park, since they could lead to dog fights, which can lead to rows with other dog owners. Leave female dogs in heat at home to avoid unwanted pregnancy. And refrain from bringing children to the run, because their behavior could incite fear or aggression in dogs, causing children to get bitten or injured.

If your dog gets involved in a fight or a deed of sexual misconduct, calmly pull the dogs apart, leash up your dog, and just go home. Never discipline a dog that is not your own. This could cause you to suffer social retribution or the doggy cold shoulder for at least a week.

Also, do not argue with other pet parents; this could escalate to a shouting match, upsetting other dogs and forcing their owners to take sides or break up a human altercation. If your dog does get hurt, exchange names and phone numbers before leaving and take your dog to the veterinarian. Best advice: work it out at a later date and away from the run, because you and your dog always use the dog run at your own risk.

If you and your dog use your neighborhood dog run on a regular basis, show your appreciation for its existence. Join the local dog run committee, spend a day helping to clean it up with other dog owners, or make a small donation for its upkeep.

By practicing your proper pet etiquette at the dog park, you and your dog will continue to socialize successfully there with other dogs and their owners.

PRODUCT RESOURCE GUIDE

To find a nearby dog park, whether you are home or traveling, visit *www.dogpark.com.*

For those times when you need to intervene, consider the Bamboo Quick Control Collar, the only dog collar with a patented, integrated, and retractable leash. Just a simple tug on the padded handles creates an instant leash for immediate control (*www.bamboopet.com*).

Chapter 12

PET PROTOCOL IN
Retail Establishments

Part of everyday living includes frequenting business establishments in your local community. The modern pet owner, especially those living in major metropolitan areas, likes to take her pet everywhere—even just on a trip to the dry cleaner. Whether you are shopping, running errands, or receiving treatment from a service provider, please be mindful of your pet manners.

BUSINESS PET POLICY

In the last few years, dogs have been allowed to accompany their owners to a myriad of stores and other business. Some establishments, like hair and nail salons as well as supermarkets, are not allowed to admit dogs, due to health codes, unless they are serving their disabled human beings. For the rest of us, health codes determine the extent of interaction between animals and humans in public, including where we can and cannot go with our pet. As a result, it is always a good idea to telephone your destination and make certain that you are welcome with your dog.

Many malls and department stores have pet policies and are happy to share them with you if you call ahead. Although you may ask the operator about visiting the store with your dog, review the policy with the store concierge, accommodations desk employee, or manager's office staff to make sure you have the pet specifics, including allowable canine size. For example, in New York, Lord & Taylor allows small dogs to be carried by their owners, preferably in a pet fashion or tote bag; while Saks Fifth Avenue will permit larger dogs to walk throughout the store accompanied by their owners.

NO MEANS NO

Occasionally we forget or don't have a chance to make contact with store personnel. If you are unsure of the pet policy, ask before entering a place of business. Whatever the response, always thank the person or staff member who has helped you. If you are denied admittance with your dog, remember that "No" means no, and your access with pooch is refused. Although you may be disappointed, maintain your cool and don't be abusive to the messenger; he is only doing his job. Your alternative is to take your dog home and come back later.

Sometimes there are occasions when we don't want to take our dog home or come back later, and we might be tempted to tie up our pet outside the store or leave him in the car. Besides being dangerous for your pet, it is inconsiderate. The fact of the matter is that it only takes a second for your dog to be stolen from either location. The presence of a dog in or near the portal of a store could also deter patrons and others from approaching the store. And if you leave him in the car, he could suffer heatstroke during the summer or freeze during the winter. Worse yet, he could chew your car upholstery or scare patrons with a barking fit as they walk by your car. Take him home or frequent stores where he can shop with you.

HOW TO SHOP TOGETHER APPROPRIATELY

While shopping together, take care that he stays with you at all times. Effectively use his leash and collar to keep him close, in a heel position. While shopping, you would be ill-advised to let him wander off lead or trail after you with his leash dragging behind him, because the immediate repercussion would be that customers could trip over his leash and seriously injure themselves. A longer aftermath is a costly legal action that could cite you and the store for negligence, pain, and suffering. So, when pet pal-ing around the store, you might want to consider a four-foot lead for better control so that he doesn't annoy other shoppers.

While in a clothing store once, I saw a woman walk in with her older bichon frisé, which wore no leash or collar and dutifully followed its master. After about twenty minutes, the customer noticed that her dog was gone. She called and called the dog, but it never appeared. At first she was overwhelmed, and then became angry with the store staff. She accused them of contributing to the theft of her dog. She was abusive and so rude to one salesgirl that the young girl ran off and cried. She even telephoned the police from her cell phone. Until the police arrived and the matter was resolved, the store owner decided to close the store down for a few hours, just until he could get the hysterical woman out.

After an hour, the old dog meandered out from a bottom shelf where it had decided to take a snooze. The dog did not hear the owner call her, because it was partially deaf and sleeping soundly. The owner was happy to find her dog, but she didn't apologize for her incredible behavior. She left in a huff, clinging to her dog. Even after she left the store, the owner did not immediately revoke his open-door pet policy; however, a few days later he finally did. It seems the old dog urinated on an expensive pair of jeans that it had slept on. I guess the owner forgot to mention that the dog was incontinent, too.

Encourage store owners to allow pets by using your well-trained and well-behaved dog as an example. If you see other pet owners abusing their right to bring their pooch along for the trip, politely remind them that they could ruin this experience for everyone and that they should appreciate the store owner's current open-door policy.

IN THE STORE

In some cases, you may not even need to walk your dog through a store. In recent years, pet strollers have become a pet owner's best friend. You can drive your pet around

PET TIP

When shopping with your dog, bring a homemade poop kit with you. A poop kit is a plastic bag that contains two paper towels. If your animal urinates or defecates on the floor or carpet, you can clean it up with one of the paper towels and throw it in the plastic bag. And, you can still have the other paper towel for another mishap.

while doing your shopping. Even better, stores like Bed, Bath & Beyond actually let you put your dog in the shopping cart and push him around with you, just like a toddler. How fun is that! But before putting your dog in the shopping cart, please check with the store management to make sure that his free ride is okay. If you do use the shopping cart, think of the next shopper by either bringing sanitizing wipes to clean the cart or laying a blanket in the wagon as a hygienic measure and a comfy place for him to rest.

WAITING IN LINE

For those places where you have to wait in line, like a bank, having your dog sitting next to you rather than lying down on the ground is a much better way for you to position him. It is much easier for a sitting dog to keep getting up as you move closer to the teller, rather than having him lie down. And you don't really want him sprawled out in line bringing attention to both of you, nor do you want a customer to step on him.

ACCIDENTS

The biggest complaint among merchants who have an open-door policy for dogs is that some of their owners refuse to pay for the merchandise that the dogs have ruined. If he does destroy something, it is your responsibility to pay for it. Like parents of two-legged kids, you must be responsible for your four-legged kid's actions.

With the admittance of dogs into a retail establishment, most shopkeepers are prepared for your dog to have an "accident." If your pet has an accident, clean it up, and either deposit the waste in an outdoor trash receptacle or flush it down the toilet in the store, because

MISS FIDO MANNERS ON . . .

Shopping at Pet Stores

Here are some tips from store owners on how to make shopping with your pet better for everyone involved:

* If your dog eliminates, don't leave pet waste in the aisles. Help clean it up or tell store personnel.

* Unless you are going to buy it, don't allow your pet to play with or eat the goods. Dog saliva contains bacteria that can be transferred to other pets and people.

* If Fido is dirty, do not try pet clothing on him. As much as we would like to believe that our dogs are practically human, their dirty fur can affect dog apparel. Bring a well-groomed dog to shop for a sweater, coat, or T-shirt—he will look better in it, too.

* Observe the return policy. Before purchasing dog stuff, review the return policy because returning items can be difficult business. Don't return items that your dog has worn a few times unless they have fallen apart or have proved to be dangerous. Best to call the store to explain what happened, then go in and speak with a manager.

you don't want unpleasant odors wafting throughout the store, disturbing other customers and staff. Also, alert the store staff, advise them where her mishap was, and assure them that you cleaned it up as best you could. Most likely, a maintenance worker will follow up and disinfect and deodorize the area.

RESIDENT PETS

There are stores that you may wish to visit that have a resident dog or other pets. For example, my dry cleaner has a troublemaking cat that teases and swats at dogs that enter her store. Once she gets them riled up, she jumps off the counter and hides, leaving the dog owners the chore of calming them down. My strategy for dealing with her is to bring her a treat so that every time she sees us, she is always on her best behavior for a stroke or a snack. As a result, my dogs are no longer subject to her shenanigans.

Obviously, this cunning won't work in every situation, but I find it best before entering an establishment that has a house dog to quickly assess your dog's personality. If your dog is aggressive toward other dogs or displays erratic behavior toward other animals, you have two choices before you enter: either politely ask the store owner to restrain her dog or other pet securely behind the counter, or come back at another time solo. If your dog is dog-friendly and well-mannered, still ask the store

116

owner, as a precautionary measure, if she and her pooch are amenable to your visit.

Upon entering the establishment, introduce the dogs before browsing or picking up your order. Some store dogs encounter so much visitor action that they prefer to lie around and not be bothered by a visiting patron and her dog. After the dogs meet and you feel that you can conduct your errand or store visit without any canine hindrance from either dog, go about your business. Under no circumstance should you take your dog off leash and let him wander around with the other dog. Most resident dogs have learned their limits, meaning they never run out of the store, and they know how to conduct themselves with new patrons coming into the store. Given the opportunity, your off-leash dog could bolt out the front door or frighten other store clients. At any time you anticipate trouble, politely ask the store personnel to put her dog behind the counter, and try to leave the store as quickly as you can so that you and your dog don't cause a disturbance or imposition.

Although we would love to take our dogs everywhere, it is not always possible. Before shopping or running errands with your four-legged friend, know the pet policies of your commercial destination so that you can anticipate how your dog will be welcomed. By being prepared, you never have to worry that your dog will be the one that causes the dog-friendly store policy to be revoked. Rather, you can just enjoy the time together and make running errands less of a chore and more fun.

PRODUCT RESOURCE GUIDE

Don't have enough hands when shopping? Push your smaller pet in a Pet Gear stroller and fill up the storage basket underneath it with the items that you need (*www.petgearinc.com*).

To find a fashionable pet carrier, browse *www.kwigy-bo.com; www.creaturecouture.com;* and *www.petote.com.*

3M Pet Care makes heavy-duty pet wipes. They are a fast and easy solution for wiping away dirt, dander, and odors (*www.3mpetcare.com*).

Chapter 13

EATING OUT WITH *Elegance*

With the challenges of confined spaces, a busy wait staff, and diners who may not have expected to share their eating experience with four-legged patrons, only the most well-mannered and best-groomed dogs should be taken out to eat at an outdoor café. Even if the state or local laws permit, al fresco dog dining is offered at a restaurant's discretion, so make sure your restaurant allows canine customers before unleashing your pet—literally or figuratively—on an unsuspecting eatery.

DINING WITH DOGS PROTOCOL

Telephone the restaurant and speak to the manager regarding their doggy dining policy. Understand that restaurants often make rules about where dogs are allowed because they must. Local health codes—which include rules about animals in restaurants—are strictly enforced by health inspectors, who can fine or even close down a restaurant for noncompliance.

Generally, dogs are allowed in outdoor dining areas, unless they have to enter the restaurant to access this area. Some restaurants allow dogs and their owners to be placed throughout the outdoor area, and others will confine you and your dog to a specific area of the patio. Then there are those restaurants that will not agree to your dog accompanying you on the terrace, but they will consent to you tying her to the rail, as long as she remains on the outside of the dining establishment on the sidewalk. Sly, aren't they? And of course, as with so many establishments these days, size may make a difference—ask the manager if there is a size restriction, too.

If you find that the policies are amenable, make a reservation. Even though your dog may be well-behaved, recognize that, like a child, the average dog may have difficulty remaining still for the duration of your meal. For this reason, consider taking your pet out for a quick lunch, light dinner, or simple snack rather than a five-course made-to-order affair—and never bring your dog to a buffet, unless you're with a companion whom you trust to get your food or watch your dog while you're away from the table.

Although restaurateurs are concerned with health codes, they are also worried about complaints from dog-less diners. So there are two rules that all pet owners must understand before visiting restaurants with companion pooches. The first is that a clean dog with a repertoire of Sit, Down, and Stay is a welcome dining pleasure, and any other type of dog is not. Therefore, the second rule is that if your dog causes a disturbance, you should be prepared to leave your meal and pay your check, which means that you should have plenty of cash on hand so that you can exit the restaurant immediately.

WHAT TO DO WHILE EATING

Once at the restaurant, request a table on the periphery. A calmer atmosphere with fewer distractions should encourage your pooch to hold a Down–Stay longer. As you approach your designated table, keep your dog close to you and under control. This is not the time to let her sniff around, explore, or, worse, greet other patrons. Once you're comfortable, instead of tying your pet's leash to the table, place the carrier—or have your dog lie down—directly under the table. Although your dog will not be noticed (and admired) by other diners, she will be safe from passing patrons and bustling servers carrying hot food or breakables, all of whom could step on a paw or tail, or trip on and injure your dog or themselves. Secure the dog by holding her leash with the hand you do not use to eat or by putting your foot through the leash loop.

As tempting as it may be to keep a small, well-trained dog on your lap during a meal, resist the urge to show her off. While you may want to display her good looks and excellent manners, or simply want to share a meal as you often do at home, it's very likely that some other customers will view this habit as unsanitary and uncouth. As pleasant a dining companion as your pooch may be to you, respect the fact that not everyone feels the same way.

Carrying pet supplies is a must for doggy diners, since it is inappropriate to allow pets to drink or eat from restaurant dinnerware. For her dining pleasure, pack a portable bowl and a few biscuits. If your pooch is thirsty, pour some water from the carafe or your glass directly into her water bowl, or have her drink from a paper cup. For restaurants that offer you a dog bowl full of water for your dog at the table, take advantage of this option; this way, you do not have to worry about disposing of your water after the meal.

NEVER FEED FROM YOUR PLATE

Once your meal is presented, don't commit a faux pas by serving her from your plate, and discourage her from begging or whining for food by discreetly giving her doggy treats—not your food—under the table.

I have a neighbor who regularly takes her dogs to the local outdoor café. She asks for a table for three, and places her Pekingese in one chair and her Lhasa Apso in the other. She feeds the dogs tidbits off her dishes, and they sit politely in their chairs throughout the meal. As adorable as it may look, not everyone wants to sit down at a table that has just been occupied by two dogs. There is dog hair on the chairs and table, and the dogs have licked the table. On one occasion, I saw a couple refuse to be seated at the table this indulgent dog owner had just vacated. The woman heard them and made an angry remark. An argument ensued. All that this does is place the restaurant owner in an extremely difficult position—and make it less likely that dogs will be welcomed in his café in the future.

PET TIP

Always take your dog for a walk and a quick play session before going out to a restaurant. The walk will ensure he doesn't need to eliminate anywhere near the restaurant, and the play session will tire him out so he will be more amenable to a long nap under your table while you are eating.

KEEP ADMIRERS AT BAY

An adorable and well-behaved dog out for a meal is sure to be an animal attraction. But don't let your canine companion cause too much of a commotion. She may get so excited that she forgets her manners. Thank her admirers for their interest and politely explain that you are famished and would like to finish your meal. On the other hand, if your server does not pet your pooch or seems to ignore her, don't be surprised. Even the slightest touch by a server requires a trip to the washroom; perhaps he can't afford to be affectionate toward your pet on his work time.

At the end of the meal, use your judgment when tipping, taking into account with whom you were dining. A tip of 20 percent is recommended when dining with your dog. If the maitre d' was helpful, thank him too. He's sure to remember you and your charming dog the next time you're hungry.

PRODUCT RESOURCE GUIDE

To find a list of restaurants that allow dogs throughout the United States and Canada, visit *www.dogfriendly.com.*

For fine, portable doggy dinnerware, consider the Sherpa travel kit at *www.sherpapet.com.*

Chapter 14

DOGGY *Demeanor*
AT THE OFFICE

People today work longer hours and spend less time enjoying the comforts of their homes. As a result, employers are always searching for innovative ways to keep employees content in the workplace. One approach to boost employee morale and productivity is to admit dogs to the workplace.

BENEFITS OF BRINGING POOCH TO WORK

In a recent study conducted by the American Pet Products Manufacturers Association (APPMA), the majority of persons polled believe that the benefits of having pets at work include relieving stress, improving relationships with coworkers, making a happier workforce, and creating an improved work environment.

According to the APPMA survey (available as a press release at *www.appma.org*):

* ✳ 55 million Americans believe having pets in the workplace leads to a more creative environment
* ✳ 53 million believe having pets in the workplace decreases absenteeism
* ✳ 50 million believe having pets in the workplace helps coworkers get along better
* ✳ 38 million believe having pets in the workplace creates a more productive work environment
* ✳ 32 million believe having pets in the workplace decreases smoking in the workplace
* ✳ 37 million believe having pets in the workplace helps improve the relationship between managers and their employees
* ✳ And, 46 million people who bring their pets to the workplace work longer hours!

But before your employer can allow you to share the daily grind with your pet, they must confirm that dogs can be admitted to the office building—especially if they don't own the facilities—and they must also assess any potential liability issues that might result. In many cases, building management companies will not allow dogs other than service dogs on the premises because if an incident occurs involving your dog, such as a dog bite, the building or your company will be subject to liability, and they could potentially be the deep-pocket players.

Muriel "Mickie" Siebert, who has been called "The First Woman of Finance," would not take no for an answer when it came bringing her dog to work with her. She is the founder and president of the New York Stock Exchange (NYSE) brokerage firm Muriel Siebert & Co. Her long list of accomplishments include becoming the first female member of the NYSE; being appointed, as a Republican, by Democratic Governor Hugh Carey in 1977 to become Super-intendent of New York State's Banking Department; writing her 2002 autobiography, *Changing the Rules—Adventures of a Wall Street Maverick*; and so much more. She loves to share her work life with her dogs, but first she had to negotiate with the landlord of her Third Avenue office building to allow her pet Chihuahua, Monster Girl, to be admitted to the workplace each

PET TIP

At mid-day, take a doggy break because the office can be a stressful place for a pet. At lunch time, give him the opportunity to eliminate and exercise by taking him for a long walk. The time out of the office will give him the opportunity to burn off some energy and you some steam.

day. Not only was she successful at that, but she was able to have Monster Girl participate in her ringing of the closing bell as an honoree of the New York Stock Exchange on January 5, 1998.

MAKING AN IMPRESSION WITH YOUR DOG AT WORK

Whether or not you had to negotiate for admission like Ms. Siebert did, if you are allowed to bring your pet to the office—for every day or for just one day of the year—recognize that having your dog at the office is a privilege not to be taken lightly. As with any office candidate, make sure that he has the right qualifications. Take your dog to the office only if he is housebroken, is friendly with strangers, and remains calm in a foreign environment. Your pooch should also be well-groomed (including being treated with an allergy-relief formula), walk nicely on a leash, and have a training repertoire of Come, Sit, and Stay. Your dog's appearance will make the first real impression when he arrives at the office, and his behavior will either confirm that he is a pleasure to work with or a real beast to be avoided at all costs.

Perhaps it is a good idea to bring your dog to the office for a "trial run." Take your dog to the office on a weekend or for a half day and make time to familiarize your dog with your workplace. On his first day of work, nothing could be worse than his pulling to greet all the staff in their offices and cubicles or urinating on your boss's leg. Even though it may be amusing to some, it's not a favorable precedent for what could be a great workday.

KEEPING EVERYONE COMFORTABLE

To ensure that you both have an enjoyable and productive day, bring his supplies of bowls, toys, treats, puppy gate, and crate or bed to the office. With his favorite things around and a puppy gate set up in the doorway of your office, he will not be distracted by the corporate hubbub and will more easily settle down with some of his own pet projects.

MISS FIDO MANNERS ON . . .

Taking Your Dog to Work

Pet Sitters International, the creator of the Take Your Dog To Work Day, is asking businesses worldwide to allow employees to bring their well-mannered dogs to the office each year in June. The event is intended to promote the human-animal bond by encouraging positive interactions between employees and canine companions. The celebration also educates individuals about the realities of pet over population. For more information, visit *www.petsit.com*.

Although everyone might like your dog at the workplace, recognize that he is your responsibility. Don't ask your assistant, a secretary, or a junior associate to take care of him. Your subordinate might feel obligated to take care of your pet for the day, but acknowledge that dog care is not part of his job description.

Should you have to leave your office or cubicle for any reason, either leave your dog in his crate or make sure, if you drag him to the meeting, that you walk him on a very short leash. Also, when riding in elevators or meeting and greeting office personnel, place your dog in a Sit–Stay. By being obedient, he will demonstrate that he is a reliable and confident team player who can follow directions.

BE CONSIDERATE OF NON-DOG-LOVERS

Although you might find it hard to believe, not everyone loves dogs. Be considerate and respectful of those who are fearful and/or allergic. Follow all office rules regarding pets, and keep dogs out of the main office, kitchen, bathrooms, or other shared common areas. If he becomes unruly, you cannot directly supervise him as necessary, or he creates a health hazard for an allergy sufferer, be prepared to take him home immediately.

PRODUCT RESOURCE GUIDE

Allerpet D cleanses a dog's hair of dander, saliva, and urine antigens considered to be the prime causes of allergic reactions people have to dogs (*www.allerpet.com*).

Carry his pet supplies in The Oval Office Adventure Tote, a lightweight tote that comes in six cool colors and is made from durable, water-resistant nylon (*www .katiesbumpers.com*).

While at work, let everyone know your dog is a genius. Have him play with Canine Genius dog toys that are durable, chewable, and stimulate his natural curiosity to hunt and to problem-solve (*www.caninegenius .com*).

PART IV

Protocol with Pet Professionals

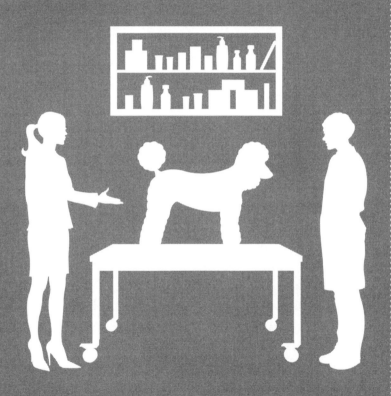

Chapter 15

VET *Esteem*

Like a good doctor, a quality veterinarian is essential to your dog's health and well-being. The best sources for finding referrals are your pet-owning friends and neighbors, or you can contact the state or local veterinary association or the American Animal Hospital Association to find a vet near you. Once you select your animal practitioner, don't forget to maintain a professional relationship. You should expect her to provide you with good service; likewise, you should treat her and her staff in a respectful manner.

CALL AROUND

If you do get a recommendation, call the doctor's office and explain that you are looking for a veterinarian to care for your dog. Try not to telephone on a Saturday because that's when these offices are at their busiest. If the receptionist requests that you call back or tells you that she will have someone call at a later time, don't be offended. Clearly and quickly give her your name and number. Before you hang up, ask for the best time to call, just in case no one responds within twenty-four hours.

Once you speak to the office personnel, ask them to send you a brochure and have them explain the pet necessities such as cost per visit, hours of operation, etc. If you are curious about their facility, don't be shy. Ask if you can have a brief tour. These days, many facilities are extremely high-tech and luxurious, and they welcome visitors.

VISIT BEFORE DECIDING

If you do visit the facility, don't bring your dog along with you. The visit is for you to figure out if the offices are clean and the staff friendly; having your pooch there could easily distract from your observations. While you are there, notice whether the office is clean, the atmosphere helps to reduce the stress of the animals, the staff handles the animals in a loving manner, and the pet owners are treated in a courteous manner. Don't be surprised if you cannot visit kennels or wards; your visit could disturb the sick or boarding animals, and your clothing might contain bacteria that could harm the animals in that sterile area.

Before leaving the office, ask if it is possible to meet one of the veterinarians on staff. Give her a few moments to check because vets, depending on the time of the day,

PET TIP

If you have pet insurance, always bring your pet claim form to your appointment and give it to the receptionist when you arrive. Before leaving the examination room, ask the vet to complete the form you left at the front desk. If you forget the insurance form, ask the receptionist if it is easier for you to fax, mail, or drop it off at the office. If you do mail it or drop it off, enclose two stamped, addressed envelopes. For faster processing, the doctor's office can send the form directly to the insurance provider and a copy of the form to you for your records.

will either be examining clients or performing surgery. If you cannot meet one of the doctors, ask if you could call at a later time or leave your telephone number and have one of the veterinarians call you back. Even if you've decided not to utilize that particular vet, always thank your tour guide for his or her time.

If the offices met your standards and you decide that you want to bring your dog there, call and schedule an appointment. Make sure to clearly state your name, telephone number, and information pertaining to your animal, including why you are seeking the veterinarian's services. Be prepared for the receptionist to put you on hold. Ask if you need to bring a stool sample or your animal's health record. Before hanging up, ask for her name just in case there is a mix-up with your appointment, and confirm your appointment time and date.

DAY OF APPOINTMENT TIPS

On the day of your visit, call a few hours early to confirm the date and the time, if the office hasn't already done so. You may wish to call to ask if appointments are operating on time. Don't be surprised if the veterinarian is running late: emergencies with other animals can always happen. Depending on the type of emergency, there is always the slight chance that the receptionist will reschedule your appointment to a later time or another date. If this is the case, be understanding, because you would expect the same treatment for your pet. On the other hand, if you are running late, telephone the office and inform them of your delayed circumstances. Ask if you can come a few minutes late or, if you are very tardy, whether you should reschedule your appointment.

If you can, try to arrive at the vet's office a few minutes early. Before entering the office, give your dog the opportunity to de-stress and eliminate. A quick walk around the block can calm her down from the excitement of the car ride, as well as give her the chance to relieve herself before sitting in a waiting room and then an examination room.

MISS FIDO MANNERS ON . . .

Second Opinions

There are times when your pet is diagnosed with a certain ailment or disease. At these times, you may want to treat your pet's health like you manage your own and seek a second opinion. Don't hesitate to ask your vet for the name of a specialist because it is not about hurting your doctor's feelings or disregarding her opinion—it's about providing your pet with the best health care possible.

Always arrive at the office with your dog on a leash or in a carrier. Introduce yourself to the receptionist and tell her the time of your appointment. Ask whether you need to complete any paperwork, and then review all paperwork for accuracy before you return it to her.

Even though you may feel impatient, sit quietly with your dog and wait your turn. Never let your pet loose to play with other animals in the waiting room. If she is nervous, try to keep her calm and quiet so as not to disturb other pets that are waiting for their appointments. Of course, there will be times when your nervous dog eliminates or vomits from the stress of the experience. If this happens, just tell the receptionist and ask if you can have paper towels and cleanser to clean up the urine or the vomit. She will probably tell you not to worry because she will either clean it up herself or have a staff member wash the floor. While you are waiting for the waste to be cleaned up, try to prevent other clients and their dogs from stepping in it.

Also, while waiting your turn, do not talk on your cell phone. Your voice could carry in the waiting room, disturbing other patients and/or their owners. If you need something to do while waiting, bring a book or your favorite magazine; this will help the time go by.

DURING THE EXAM

When you leave the waiting room and meet the veterinarian, introduce yourself and your dog. Tell her how you were referred to her, because many vet offices send thank-you notes to their referral sources. Clearly state why you are seeking her services (e.g., routine appointment, eye problem, more frequent urination, weight loss) and try to make your statement informative and concise. Before visiting the vet, it can help to make a list of the ailments that are bothering your pet so that you can remember more easily once there.

Take a seat while the doctor is examining her. Don't talk through the examination unless the vet questions you. Having your vet free of distractions gives her the ability to listen to your dog's heart and pulse, helping her to better to assess your dog's health. If your dog is agitated on the examination table, ask your vet what you can do to help. In most cases, a veterinarian would rather use a veterinary technician to hold the patient, but she might suggest that you stand up or move to a certain place so that the dog can see you. If they are having difficulty restraining your dog, or need to perform blood work or other tests, they might take your dog off to another room. Don't be alarmed. Let the veterinarian and her staff do their jobs. Ask where they are going and why, and then sit patiently and wait.

During the appointment, be sure to listen carefully to what the doctor says, including any recommendations she makes. If at any time you do not understand what she is saying to you, say "Excuse me" and ask for a point of clarification. Do not be upset if she asks you to repeat yourself or asks questions similar to the information that you have provided her. Remember, she is trying to determine the best course of treatment for your animal. If she decides to prescribe any medication, always ask about side effects, as they could affect you as well as your dog. For example, some medications might make your animal thirsty and urinate more frequently so you might have to adjust her walking schedule. Other medications could make her sleepy and lethargic; knowing all of the side effects in advance will save you worry later on if your dog is acting out of sorts.

AFTER THE APPOINTMENT

At the end of your appointment, thank the doctor for her time. Wait patiently for your medication to be dispensed and your bill to be prepared. Before leaving, review the medication requirements with the vet technician and, if necessary, book another appointment. Review your bill thoroughly and be prepared to pay it in full.

If a friend or neighbor referred you to your new veterinarian, telephone him to thank him, or send him a note showing your appreciation.

VET-IQUETTE

Emergencies. There could be a time that you will have an emergency with your pet. Hysteria is just par for the course, but if you are prepared, you will be better behaved. If your vet offers twenty-four-hour emergency service, acquaint yourself with their policies. Do you call and wait for someone to call you back? Do you just bring your pet to the office in middle of the night and have the vet technician call the veterinarian on call? If your vet does not offer emergency or twenty-four-hour services, ask her office early on what hospital you should visit after hours. Make sure you keep the telephone number of that facility's address in your first-aid kit, too. Call the twenty-four-hour emergency facility and ask what their procedures are in advance so that you will be prepared to handle any situation.

Death and paying your bill in full. Many doctors complain that if a dog patient dies, clients sometimes refuse to pay them. This is just poor taste. If your dog does die, it is your obligation to pay your veterinarian. If you believe that she has handled your pet's health in a negligent manner, pursue the matter through the correct regulatory or legal channels.

Payment plans. If you are confronted with an extremely expensive course of treatment, ask your veterinarian what payment options are available to you. Often, if you are a good client, your veterinarian will allow you to work out a payment plan. If she does, work with the office manager to come up with a timely schedule of payments and stick to it. Once you pay your bill in full, send your veterinarian a thank-you note or small gift, such as a flower arrangement, to let her know that you appreciated her kindness.

Such a need for a payment plan arose for Christopher, who, with his dog, Scooby, was always a good client of New York veterinarian Dr. Sherman. Scooby was a favorite patient of the office staff and technicians, always making them smile by kissing them after every visit—his way of thanking them for being gentle and pleasant. His owner was also a dream client, always understanding if appointments ran late or medical emergencies happened while they were in the office.

As Scooby aged, Chris sought more advice and medical treatments for his pet's kidney problems. After every visit, he thanked the doctor and staff for making his older dog feel as comfortable as possible and he always paid his bill in full. One fall day, Chris called the office, frantic because Scooby was very ill. Ultimately, Scooby needed costly emergency surgery. Although embarrassed, he asked Dr. Sherman if he could work out a payment plan, because he just couldn't swing the layout of that much cash at that time. Because of his good relationship with the practice and his payment history, Dr. Sherman granted his request. Although Scooby made full recovery from the surgery, within a few months he died. On the day he picked up Scooby's ashes, Chris sent Dr. Sherman and the office staff lunch—on Scooby—because they were always so kind to both of them.

PRODUCT RESOURCE GUIDE

American Animal Hospital Association members that choose to become AAHA-accredited hospitals have challenging standards to meet. To find an AAHA hospital near you or close to where you are traveling, visit *www.healthypet.com*.

When it comes to canine safety, preventive measures are important. Since accidents can happen any time, have a first-aid kit handy to treat canine emergencies (*www.ruffwear.com*).

It is always a good idea to keep your veterinarian's telephone number and the number of the ASPCA Poison Control Center (1-888-4-ANI-HELP) in your pet's first-aid kit.

If you are thinking about pet insurance, contact Veterinary Pet Insurance, the nation's oldest and largest provider of health insurance for pets. Pet insurance helps to pay for pets' office visits, surgeries, x-rays, lab fees, and much more. For information, visit *www.petinsurance.com*.

Chapter 16

TAKING CARE OF
PET *Nannies*

These days it is not uncommon for your boss to inform you at 6:00 p.m. that you are leaving the next day for a week-long business trip. Unfortunately, your new Brussels Griffon doesn't get a ticket, and your mother is unavailable to care for her granddog. Besides, with your crazy work schedule, you have used up all of your favors with your best friend for the month. The answer is to find a "pet nanny," a loving, educated, responsible pet-care provider who understands that your dog means the world to you, and who can also keep up with your hectic schedule. In return for her understanding and excellent service, you should pay her well and treat her with dignity.

FINDING AND PREPARING A SITTER
To search for a person to care for your four-legged kid, you can call your veterinarian and ask for a referral,

or contact the National Association of Professional Pet Sitters or Pet Sitters International to find pet-care providers near you. When interviewing a sitter, notice whether she treats your pet in a firm, loving manner and ask if she is trained in animal-handling skills and first aid. Even though your dog may take an instantaneous liking to her, remember that this person is also spending time in your home. Confirm that she is bonded, insured, and has at least three references. She should be willing to completely care for your pet while you're way, even if that means cooking scrambled eggs for his breakfast.

PET TIP

When interviewing a pet sitter, always confirm that she has a contingency plan, should she become ill or have a situation that prohibits her from caring for your pet.

Once you find a choice pet sitter—one you and your dog both feel comfortable with—prepare her for the job. Introduce her to one of your neighborhood friends, explaining that she will be visiting your home while you are away and there's no need to worry if the lights are on or if someone is coming in and out of your home. If you live in an apartment building, have her also meet the doorman from whom she will be obtaining keys. Make sure to review community or building regulations, such as dog-walking paths or service elevators that she should use when with your pet.

To make her job as easy as possible, always leave your pet-care provider your specific 411, the information that she can use to best take care of your dog. Your detailed instructions should include his dislikes and likes, appropriate feeding instructions, walking routes, and emergency instructions. Always leave her your veterinarian's telephone number and the number of a relative or neighbor. Don't forget, an updated itinerary with all of your contact telephone numbers should be left in a prominent place, like on a kitchen counter or attached with a magnet to the refrigerator.

Before you leave for your vacation or business trip, put all appropriate supplies and equipment out for your pet sitter on the kitchen counter or other convenient place. Shop for more than enough food, treats, and poop bags, just in case you have to remain away for a few more days than planned. It is always a good idea to check leashes and collars and replace any old or worn ones that might decide to break while you're away. Who would even want to think about the horrible consequences should your dog get away, get lost, or become injured because of faulty equipment? Also, leave a small sum of money for emergencies and the name and location of the local pet store, should your pet sitter need additional supplies.

If you're so inclined, you can ask your pet sitter to pen a note to you about your dog's daily activities while you are away. This way, you can confirm that he is receiving the care for which you contracted.

MISS FIDO MANNERS ON . . .
Dog Walkers

Unlike a pet sitter who comes to your home to take care of your pet when you are on a business trip or a vacation, a dog walker is a pet professional who will walk your dog, either while you are at work five days a week or at random times on an as-needed basis. When hiring a dog walker, use the same criteria as you would with a pet sitter, and expect the same level of professionalism. Generally, dog-walker compensation is left for them at the end of the work week or after an isolated job is performed. Tipping your dog walker is a recommended "thank you" at least once a year, preferably during the holiday season or at times that you feel it is appropriate. Two weeks' salary, presented in cash in a holiday card, is an appropriate gift from you; a picture frame, candle, or hat and scarf is a great optional gift from your dog.

ADDITIONAL REQUESTS

Should you cancel your trip or return early, be mindful and considerate of your pet caregiver's time. Try to cancel at least twenty-four hours in advance. If you do not, expect to pay for services that you did not use. In most cases, pet sitters will have service contracts spelling out all the particulars, including a cancellation policy with which you are obligated to comply.

If you need your pet professional to perform additional services, such as taking your dog to the groomer or veterinarian or shopping for pet supplies, ask politely and offer to pay an additional amount for her time. Don't forget to thank her for fulfilling your request.

Remember to always pay your pet sitter in a timely manner. Tipping your pet professional is par for the course. Gratuities of 15 to 20 percent are appropriate per job and a small holiday gift is appropriate for a regular sitter.

Andrew, a very busy executive who often traveled at a moment's notice, had hired Lisette as a dog walker and nanny because she had stellar credentials, impeccable references, and his dog, Sammie, adored her. While Andrew was on a business trip to Asia, Lisette noticed that pieces of plaster had fallen from his ceiling. She immediately called Andrew and left him a message that she thought there might be a problem with his ceiling and that it would be advisable for him to call the building superintendent or a contractor to deal with this potential problem ASAP. Only a few days later, when Lisette opened Andrew's condo door she found that his ceiling had collapsed, ruining thousands of dollars' worth of furnishings, artwork, and personal belongings. She immediately called every number left on his itinerary, including his secretary's number, and explained the situation. Unfortunately, Andrew was involved in a complex business deal and could not return home immediately. He asked Lisette if she could "handle" things while he was away, such as taking Sammie to a friend's home to stay and taking a few pictures of the damage to e-mail to him so that he could contact his insurance company. Lisette agreed, because she knew her job as a pet sitter not only included caring for her client's pet, but also keeping a watchful eye on his home. And, because of her thoughtfulness and consideration, Andrew rewarded her with a bonus for her beyond-the-call-of-duty attitude and actions.

WHY HIRE A SITTER?

Hiring a professional pet sitter is a viable option for pet owners traveling for business or pleasure. While you are away, your dog can be comfortable in his own home and your sitter can provide him with his regular routine of diet and exercise. With this in-home pet-care solution, you will no longer have to rely on family, friends, or neighbors to take care of your baby while you are away.

PRODUCT RESOURCE GUIDE

The National Association of Professional Pet Sitters (*www.petsitters.org*) or Pet Sitters International (*www.petsit.com*) can help you find a professional pet sitter to care for your pet when you are away from home.

Planet Dog has created a notebook of pet sitting instructions. The fill-in-the-blank sections allow you to include emergency numbers, special instructions, and more. See *www.planetdog.com.*

Chapter 17

BEING *Gracious* WITH GROOMERS

When buying a dog—especially one of the more popular breeds, such as a Shih Tzu, Soft-Coated Wheaten terrier, or even a designer dog such as a Malti-poo (Maltese-poodle mix)—a new pet owner must calculate the cost of monthly grooming into her budget. If your dog is a permanent fixture in your home, regular grooming is necessary to keep your pet clean and your home tidy. Developing a relationship with a good groomer is paramount to achieving these goals.

Although all dogs need brushing, combing, and bathing, some dogs need more grooming than others. Depending on the type of dog you have, consider the amount of grooming that your breed will need and whether you can take care of her needs at home or prefer to have them done by a professional. Some dogs, like Boston terriers and basenji, shed very little and require no professional grooming. Other dogs, like bichon frisés, poodles, and Cairn terriers, shed very little but need hand-scissoring, clipping, and hand-stripping to make them look their best. While golden retrievers and Dalmatians shed constantly and do not require professional grooming, bearded collies, springer spaniels, and Shetland sheepdogs all shed and need regular and professional grooming. Most dogs should be groomed every four to six weeks; with an average price of about $60.00 per grooming, these costs can add up wherever you decide to have your dog beautified.

FIND A GROOMER AND MAKE AN APPOINTMENT

Pet grooming can be found in specialized shops, pet stores, a veterinarians' offices, mobile vans, and groomers' homes. Some groomers even make house calls. To obtain a referral for an excellent dog groomer, ask your veterinarian or pet-owning neighbors, or browse *www .findagroomer.com*. Before hiring a pet stylist, discuss his education. While some groomers attend grooming school, others have been self-taught, study with breeders, or work with dog handlers for the show ring. Moreover, verify that the groomer is licensed in those states with licensing requirements and that he carries liability insurance. And, before leaving your pet anywhere, look around to see if the groomer and the salon are clean and the dogs in his care are treated well.

Once you have done your research and found a groomer that you like, schedule an appointment. While on the telephone with the shop receptionist, ask all relevant questions so there are no surprises when you pick up your pet. Inquire about the length of your pet's grooming appointment, the necessary drop-off and pickup times, and the cost, including any additional charges for a matted coat or advanced styling.

PET TIP

To keep your pet looking her best, schedule a standing monthly appointment (e.g., the first Tuesday of the month). This way you will never have to worry that at the busiest times of the year, like Christmas, you will not receive service.

If your pet is matted, in most cases she will need to be stripped. Stripping is shaving your pet down, leaving very little hair. Think of it as giving your pet a crew cut. In that particular situation, some groomers will make you sign a release before they commence giving her this cut. Don't be upset; realize that you can avoid this happening again by caring for your pet's coat on a regular basis. Remember, hair always grows back. For dogs like a standard poodle, advanced styling is a must. Quality hand-scissoring takes years to master, and, like a premium New York City or L.A. hairstylist, be assured that a top dog stylist is going to cost you, too!

Before your appointment, be honest about your dog. If she is a nervous nipper, doesn't like to be caged, or detests strangers, reveal her unique personality to the grooming staff. Remember, no surprises! Of course, the grooming staff should be prepared for any situation, but giving them all pertinent information will make the job of handling your dog easier and contribute to a less stressful experience for her.

Sometimes things come up that force us to cancel appointments. Should you need to cancel her grooming appointment, try to notify the groomer at least twenty-four hours in advance. One of the biggest complaints of groomers is that clients book the time and never show up for the appointments, especially on rainy days. So be considerate, and give the groomer more than enough time to book another client in your place. If it is raining, don't cancel your appointment—just bring a raincoat when you pick her up.

APPOINTMENT DAY

On the morning of your appointment, it is ill-advised to send your pet to the groomer with a stomach full of food. Feed her only a small snack or light meal. This will ensure that her morning hunger is satisfied, but it will reduce the possibility of her vomiting and requiring the grooming staff to spend time cleaning up rather than making her look beautiful.

Once you arrive at the facility, give your dog a brisk walk as an opportunity to eliminate. Upon entering, introduce yourself and your pooch to the receptionist. Complete any necessary paperwork, and remind them of your pet's likes and dislikes. Discuss your pet's styling and the condition of her coat. Should you agree that your dog needs to be stripped when the weather is cold, make sure you bring a coat or sweater so that she can be warm when you pick her up. Before leaving the shop, ask what time your dog will be finished. Call before you pick her up, and if you are going to be late, apologize and tell them your estimated time of arrival.

WHAT A GROOMING ENTAILS

A good grooming session entails a variety of steps to keep your dog looking her best. First, a thorough brushing and combing of your dog's coat will remove any dead hair and mats. Next, a groomer will clean your dog's ears by applying a medicated powder that will stiffen the hairs so they can be plucked out with his fingers. The eyes and, if necessary, facial folds will be cleaned with a damp piece of cotton. The nails will be cut and the hair around the rectal area, the groin area, and the paw pads will be clipped. In most cases, a groomer will perform a rough cut, followed by a good bathing. He will either fluff or cage-dry your dog, depending upon her coat. After she is dried, the groomer will continue to clip your dog into the recommended breed style. The finishing touches to the face and feet will be completed by a good thinning shear and hand-scissoring. In most cases, a finishing spray will help her fur to glisten. Afterwards, a good groomer will let his client know of any unusual lumps, bumps, discharges, or odors. Take his recommendations seriously for better pet health.

Although some groomers express anal glands, others do not. (Anal glands are the kidney-shaped glands on each side of the anus that usually release on their own; if they don't, they can become clogged and possibly infected. If they emit a pungent odor, that indicates they need to be emptied.) In general, the smaller dog breeds and the low-shedding breeds such as poodles have a problem with blocked anal glands more than any other breeds. I believe that it is better to have the emptying procedure done by a veterinarian rather than a groomer because it is a medical procedure, not a cosmetic one. On those days that you have the procedure done, either have your dog bathed at the vet's before she returns home, or take her to a groomer afterward for a good washing because the extracted liquid could penetrate the dog's hair, causing your pet to smell unpleasant.

AFTER THE APPOINTMENT

When you pick up your dog after her appointment, ask for the groomer who styled your dog so that you can thank him and present him with a gratuity of 15 percent. If your groomer is gone for the day, leave the tip in a sealed envelope with his name, your name, and the name of your dog. When you are finished paying the bill, take your dog out and let her do her business. If your grooming shop is a boutique, too, come back and shop after she has had a chance to relieve herself. If your dog has an accident before departing, apologize and offer to clean it up. Most likely, a staff member will mop up for you.

Remember, a little graciousness goes a long way. Always treat your groomer with consideration, because he is part of your pet's health management team, too. During the holidays, the price of one grooming is appropriate for a holiday gift for your groomer. If you frequent the shop on a regular basis and a few staff members take part in your dog's styling, purchase a group gift, like a basket full of savories. Always enclose a card with a handwritten message acknowledging your appreciation of their care and styling of your dog.

Amanda was glad that she had a good relationship with her groomer when she noticed that Max, her standard schnauzer, was scratching his neck and the side of his head more than usual. Amanda thought that the dog had fleas, because she had recently taken him to the country for a weekend outing. Worried that her home would also become flea-infested, she called her groomer and asked if Max could be scheduled immediately for a flea bath. Magda, her groomer for five years, fit her in the next day. Once she got a confirmation from Magda, she also arranged for an exterminator to visit her home the same day. An hour after she dropped Max off, Magda called to let Amanda know that Max did not have fleas but rather a bad ear infection. She advised Amanda to pick up Max and take him to the vet to seek medical treatment. When Amanda picked him up, she asked Magda how she knew. Magda replied that part of the grooming session includes cleaning his ears, and that a good groomer should be familiar with a dog's physique and should be able to detect possible health problems.

PRODUCT RESOURCE GUIDE

Search *www.findagroomer.com* to find a dog groomer near you.

To keep your dog's coat in optimal condition, use Bamboo's brush and combo combination tools at *www.bamboopet.com*.

Chapter 18

HANDLING *Dog Trainers* WELL

Receiving a quality pet education taught by a good dog-training instructor is nothing to bark at. A good dog-obedience instructor will teach you how you can train your dog on your own. She will explain and demonstrate techniques that you can apply in your daily life to have a well-mannered dog. As you would with any professor, remember to treat your teacher with respect.

FINDING THE RIGHT TRAINER AND PROGRAM

Find a good dog trainer by discussing your training needs with your veterinarian. Either he can provide you with a worthy referral or you can dig up one by browsing the Web sites of the Association of Pet Dog Trainers, the National Association of Dog Obedience Instructors, or the International Association of Canine Professionals.

Dog obedience courses are generally one-hour sessions for six to eight weeks, with a basic training program designed to teach your dog to Come, Sit, Stay, Lie Down, and Heel. There are also intermediate and advanced training classes that build upon fundamental skills, with a focus on off-leash behavior, games, and agility, and some classes for owners interested in competitive obedience. Some schools also offer therapy classes for those who want to volunteer their pets in schools, hospitals, and convalescent homes. A relatively new concept is puppy kindergarten, which promotes loving interaction and socialization with your young pup. This class includes housebreaking within its lesson plans.

When choosing a program, be sure to ask about the instructor's teaching methods—seek training with a positive, not punitive, approach to educating your pet. Most importantly, observe a class to see how your instructor interacts with the students and their dogs. If you don't have the opportunity to watch a class, ask for at least three references and contact them.

Once you've found a program or school that you like, you will be required to pay the tuition in full and complete an enrollment form with your contact information and your pet's particulars. Although you have completed your paperwork and paid, you will not be allowed to enter class unless you have supplied the school with proof of your dog's vaccinations and rabies inoculation. Simply call your vet a few days in advance for a health certificate and bring it on the first day of class. Moreover, check the class brochure or Web site or call the instructor so that you attend class with the proper equipment. Most likely, you will need to bring either a flat or martingale-style collar (a type of collar that a dog wears loose and tightens only when it needs to be tight for gentle, pet-owner control), a six-foot lead (no retractable leashes, please), poop bags for cleanup, and your dog's favorite treats.

CLASS TIME

On the first day of class and thereafter, arrive a few minutes early with a clean dog and give your dog an opportunity to eliminate. If he does have an accident inside the training area, clean it up with your poop bags and dispose of the waste in the appropriate trash receptacle. If your class is indoors, in all likelihood you will also have to wipe the floor with the school-supplied paper towels, cleanser, and mop. Clean up as quickly as possible so that you do not delay the class and you can get back to the fun.

While the teacher is lecturing or demonstrating, pay attention and try to refrain from talking to your classmates or having your dogs play together. If you need to ask a question, politely raise your hand or interrupt her by saying, "Excuse me. I have a question." During the practice exercises, wait patiently for the instructor to come over to review your progress; recognize that she has only a few minutes to spend with each dog and owner before moving on to the next student and his dog. If you continue to have trouble getting enough time for your concerns to be addressed, ask if she has a few minutes to work with you after class or before the next class, the following week.

Many dog-training instructors also offer phone instruction in conjunction with their training program to students who need a little extra advice. If her scheduled phone time is inconvenient for you, ask if you can call her at a more opportune time for your schedule. If she agrees to a set time, make sure not to miss the appointment. Take into consideration that these mini phone training sessions should last no more than five to ten minutes.

HOMEWORK

In most educational settings, instructors don't buy the excuse that your dog ate your homework, but in dog-training class, you could probably get away with that defense. If your dog does destroy your homework, call the instructor to obtain another syllabus and ask for guidance about doggy paper shredding. Between classes you need to practice and come to the next class prepared. Without working between sessions, you can hinder your progress, because some commands are used as building blocks for others. For example, once your dog has mastered the "Sit," it will be easier to teach him "Down" from a sitting position.

KEEP IN TOUCH

At the end of the class, thank the instructor. If you really enjoyed the class, you can give her a token of your appreciation. Discreetly give her your present at the end of the last session so as not to embarrass the dog owners who didn't bring gifts. Make sure you have included a handwritten note from you and your dog thanking her for the experience. And don't forget to get her business card. Safeguard her contact information—just in case you have a problem later on in your dog's life and you need to consult with her.

PET TIP

Safeguard your dog-training materials by keeping them in a binder. If, at a later date, your dog is having behavioral problems, you can refer to them for help.

Although Betsy didn't take dog training classes, she had such a successful experience working privately with a dog trainer, Denise, that she always sang the trainer's praises. Betsy had had enormous difficulties housebreaking her Tibetan terrier puppy, Lulu, on her own; she even thought Lulu had a health problem, so she took her to the veterinarian. After a thorough examination, Lulu was given a clean bill of health and Betsy was given Denise's name to help her with Lulu's housebreaking. Within a few weeks of working with Denise, Betsy saw remarkable improvements with her dog. Soon after, Lulu was housebroken. Over the years, Betsy kept in touch with Denise by sending her referrals of pet owners who needed dog training. So when Lulu's problem resurfaced after a move to a new apartment, Betsy called Denise for help. Denise, thankful for the referrals, rearranged her schedule and came the next day to help Lulu solve her housebreaking problems. Denise reviewed the housebreaking basics that she taught Betsy so many years before. She had Betsy buy a new crate and put Lulu on a feeding, watering, and walking schedule. Within a few weeks, Lulu returned to eliminating outside. It pays off to be a teacher's pet!

As it did for Lulu, no matter the age or breed of your dog, training always has a positive effect. To make the most out of your experience with your instructor, you might need to call on her a few times throughout the life of your dog, so work hard, do your homework, and try to make a good impression.

PRODUCT RESOURCE GUIDE

To find a dog trainer near you, visit the Web sites of the Association of Pet Dog Trainers (*www.apdt.com*), the International Association of Canine Professionals (*www.dogpro.org*), or the National Association of Obedience Instructors (*www.nadoi.org*).

To find training collars, leads, head collars, and a treat pouch, visit *www.premier.com*.

Chapter 19

Good Manners AT
BOARDING KENNELS

The outdated version of a boarding kennel is a facility
of outbuildings composed of make-shift rooms constructed of chicken wire, wood, and concrete and
covered with aluminum roofs. To the modern pet, this
idea is nothing more than doggy jail, where innocent
pooches are sentenced for the duration of their owner's vacation or business trip. Now, boarding kennels
are state-of-the-art facilities with climate-controlled
rooms, luxury bedding and accoutrements, gourmet
health food, and a staff of animal-care specialists to
wait on your pampered puppy night and day. A big
spender can book his dog in a private, deluxe suite,
with a television and VCR playing movies like *101
Dalmatians* and nature films. Although your nearest boarding kennel may not be like the one I just
described, the idea is that while you are gone, your
dog will have a great time away from home.

FINDING AND BOOKING A KENNEL

When looking for a boarding kennel, speak to your veterinarian and your dog-owning friends, or browse the Web site of the American Boarding Kennel Association for a member kennel near you. Telephone the kennel and ask about the pet particulars, such as pet housing, feeding procedures, exercise regime, and veterinary affiliation in the event your pet becomes ill or injured. Additionally, inquire about ancillary services, such as pickup and delivery, grooming, training, and playtime options. Also, review what should accompany your pet to the facility, including a favorite toy or blanket.

Before your dog is admitted to the facility, you will need to provide proof of up-to-date vaccinations, including a required Bordetella shot to prevent kennel cough. Kennel cough is an infection that can damage and irritate the lining of your dog's trachea and upper bronchial tubes. It is usually contracted when a large group of dogs are together in one environment like a kennel.

It is always a good idea to visit a kennel, just to make sure it's as good as it looks on the Web site and as good as it sounds from the staff's description. Your sneak peek can confirm that the facility meets your standard of care, and that the environment is conducive to your dog's needs.

While on site, determine whether the facility is clean and well-maintained; note whether the front desk staff is professional and treats pet owners, including you, hospitably. Observe how the staff treats the dogs and whether the dogs are having a good time. Don't be surprised if you are barred from the barracks or sleeping accommodations. Your visit to those areas could either transmit bacteria and viruses or upset the animals. If there is a viewing window or a television monitor showing the kennel area, be content with that.

PET TIP

The best boarding kennels are booked weeks, and sometimes months, in advance of holidays and summer vacation months. When you know of vacation, business, or holiday plans, be sure to call the kennel and reserve a space as early as possible.

YOUR DOG'S STAY

If you like what you've seen, have a doggy trial run before leaving your dog for a longer stay. Make arrangements for your dog to have a mini-break or weekend stay. Prior to her leaving home, send the kennel your complete itinerary, with all telephone numbers; her health records, including your veterinarian's telephone number; feeding and/or medication instructions; and other relevant information, including a short description of your dog's personality, likes, and dislikes. Any information about your dog will always help the kennel staff take better care of her.

On the day of her departure, don't feed her a big meal in the morning. The ride could upset her stomach. Keep to her regular routine: walk her, kiss her, pet her, and send her on her way—off for a fun weekend.

MISS FIDO MANNERS ON . . .
Doggy Daycare

Doggy daycare is a lot like daycare for toddlers. In many urban environments, the facilities can even send a shuttle van to pick her up and drop her off each day. For professionals working long hours, it is a comfort to not have to leave your pet home alone, especially if she is destructive, very active, or just in need of some company. But after you have screened a facility and determined that it is good and safe enough for your pet, she still has to be admitted into the program, just like a human kid. Candidates are temperament-tested before they are allowed to join the facility's playgroups. She will meet with a counselor, and then be evaluated for how well she plays with others. Dogs that are aggressive will be immediately declined admission. It just goes to show you: good behavior and social skills matter.

If she is a social butterfly in need of interaction, or an adolescent dog that likes to play rough with the other doggies, add group playtime. But if your dog is shy and needs some tender loving care, consider a solo session, where she can be adored by the loving staff member who will play with her and make her feel special without the distraction of other dogs. For really pampered princesses—and if the services are offered—buy a spa package, too. Many places offer aromatherapy, massage, and other treatments that you might wish you were having instead of your dog. She will enjoy the treatments, and the health benefits will contribute to a more relaxed dog in a new environment. For dogs in need of a refresher course in manners, sign her up with a tutor to review the dog-training basics. Dog training at the facility can be stimulating and enjoyable while she is away from home. Another perk of the dog-training sessions is that she can receive some one-on-one interaction with a staff member. Before booking services, speak to the dog trainer to review his training methodology, as well as what specific skills your dog is having a problem with.

RETURN TRIP

You can arrange for your dog to be bathed on the last morning of her stay. A good grooming will ensure that she comes home smelling fresh and clean and not like the kennel. That morning, call the kennel and ask about her stay, confirming her estimated time of arrival if you contracted for transportation services. Once she is home, observe her behavior. If she seems upset, call the kennel management office immediately; but if she seems calm, walks into the house, and relaxes on her bed, you can be sure she had a good time but is glad to be home.

MISS FIDO MANNERS ON . . .

Tipping Practices at Kennel Services

Because of my rigorous travel schedule, I have to have many pet-care options for my animals. For longer trips, I leave my dogs at a country kennel. Although the kennel provides transportation services, I always tip the driver a few dollars for driving my babies to and from the kennel safely. When my dogs see him, they greet him enthusiastically and immediately walk with him to the back of the shuttle bus. Over the years, I have developed a relationship with the bather, trainer, and playtime activities coordinator, and I seasonally tip them, because they always take excellent care of my dogs. And because I use the facility many times during the course of the year, I have a nice holiday lunch brought in for the kennel staff from a nearby restaurant once a year.

Henry, an avid traveler, considers himself very fortunate to have found a great boarding kennel for his dog, Harry, a fun-loving curly-coated retriever. Harry has such a great time at the kennel, he sometimes has a hard time leaving. When Henry returns from his trips he is always pleased, because Harry is lively and happy to see him. For a minute, when Harry realizes that he is going home, the dog always runs back and forth between Henry and the kennel owner. The dog sometimes grabs the sleeve of the kennel owner and tries to drag her toward the door as if to say, "Why can't she come home with us, Dad?"

Like Harry's, the modern boarding kennel wants to provide your pet with an exciting and stimulating environment while she is away from home, and you with the comforting knowledge that while you are traveling your pet is safe and being treated well. As with any good experience, thank the kennel in writing for treating your dog like the princess she is, and refer the name and number of the boarding kennel to her royal court of friends.

PRODUCT RESOURCE GUIDE

Before sending her off to the boarding kennel, make sure that she is protected from fleas and ticks (*www.frontline.com*) and has heartworm prevention (*www.ah.novartis.com*).

Send your dog to the kennel with rubber toys that are fun and easy to clean (*www.kongcompany.com*).

For her comfort when she is away from home, consider one of the easy-to-wash West Paw Design Dog Mats (*www.westpawdesigns.com*).

Whether you have a big dog or a small dog, it is always a good idea to have the multipurpose Sherpa bag. Although it is designed to carry small dogs on planes, I like to use it as a doggy suitcase, too. It is big enough for a five-pound pack of food, toys, and sleeper mat. Store medications and your instructions in the side pockets (*www.sherpapet.com*).

PART V

Travel, Sports, and Leisure

Chapter 20

Best Guest BEHAVIOR

If you receive an invitation for a weekend away, only ask about bringing your dog with you if the host is a close family member or a very dear friend. A great weekend is one in which everyone has a good time, so if you believe that your dog will be well-behaved and not detract from the weekend, bring him along and enjoy yourself.

A few years ago, I got a telephone call from a training client asking for my advice. She told me that her mother was beside herself because her brother's fiancée was insisting on bringing her poorly trained Maltese to their weekend beach house on Long Island's Hamptons. I advised that her mother should sit down with her son and his soon-to-be bride and discuss the problem. She should maintain that the dog will only be welcome in her home if the couple works with a dog trainer to devise a feeding, watering, and walking schedule; confines the dog to a crate; and do a better job supervising the pooch while at the house on the weekends. To let them know how serious she was, the mother offered to pay for their dog training, if they would hire me. I ended up working with the couple at their home, and even at the mother's beach home. Now, the family is very happy to be together on the weekends. The mother was even proud to have her new granddog at her son's wedding, meeting her friends.

TO BRING OR NOT TO BRING YOUR DOG

Although he may be your dearest boy, if he barks when left alone, is not people-friendly, is aggressive toward other dogs, is a destructive chewer, and, to tell the truth, is not really housebroken, then either decline the invitation and stay home or accept the invitation and leave your badly behaved dog with a pet sitter or book him into kennel camp for an attitude adjustment. If your dog is housebroken, can make new friends easily, adjusts to new environments, and listens to verbal commands, consider asking your host if you can bring your pooch along.

If you get turned down, don't be displeased. Accept that there are people who like dogs but don't want them as visitors in their home; there are also those who suffer from allergies. Please don't try to convince your host or pressure her with "a love me, love my dog" attitude. Frankly, this behavior is inappropriate and impolite and may just get your own invitation revoked. But if your host grants your dog an invitation, immediately discuss the doggy details.

DOGGY DETAILS

Tell your host about your pet's personality and habits. If your dog eliminates on paper and training pads (specially treated absorbent pads that puppies or dogs relieve themselves on), ask to stay in a room with a bathroom where you can easily clean the floor. If your pet likes to lounge on the furniture, tell her that he will jump off if ordered. And if she has a pet, ask about his disposition. You might even suggest that she pick up her dog's toys so as to prevent a quarrel. Who wants to spend the weekend pulling apart dogs that are fighting? Unlike with children, you can get bitten and need medical attention. If your host has children and they are small, remind her that constant supervision is the key when dogs and children are together. All in all, if you can come to terms about your visit, then accept the invitation and look forward to having a good time.

MAKING YOUR DOG COMFORTABLE

Before leaving home, pack up your pet's food, crate or puppy gate, toys, bowls, and a plastic place mat. If your dog likes to sleep in bed with you, bring a sheet or blanket to prevent shedding and soiling, and don't forget an odor eliminator and stain product just in case your pooch has an accident. Especially if there is another dog in the house, there is a good chance that your male will "mark" a chair or piece of furniture within the first thirty minutes of visiting. If an accident happens, apologize, and clean it up immediately. If necessary, offer to pay for the furniture cleaning.

Once in your guest room, unpack and organize your pet's possessions. This strategy helps him adjust and calm down more quickly, as he will develop a more secure demeanor in a strange place if he knows where to eat and drink, go to the bathroom, and relax.

If there is another dog in the house, have them meet as soon as possible, preferably outside on loose leads. If they seem to get along, take them off lead and let them play in an enclosed area. Within a few minutes, have them

PET TIP

Before visiting a friend with your dog, find the name of a nearby kennel or pet sitter, in case you have a problem that involves needing to find him different lodging arrangements.

enter the house and continue to observe their behavior. If at any time either dog displays any seriously aggressive behavior, separate them. Hopefully, they will get along fabulously, but when you leave the house, confine them in different rooms as a precautionary measure.

KEEPING A NORMAL SCHEDULE

While visiting friends, always try to balance your dog's regular schedule with the house activities, which could mean feeding him earlier or walking him at different times of the day. When you have a chance, take your dog out for a long walk, because this will give him the opportunity to spend some alone time with you. Ask your host about the best places to walk your dog: if there is a country trail or a dog-friendly beach, take advantage of the opportunity to give your dog a new experience and meet some other friendly dogs. If your host suggests walking your dog in the neighborhood, ask about the possibility of encountering loose unfriendly dogs. Depending upon her answer, it might be in your best interest to play fetch with your dog in the yard, as long as your playing doesn't wake up the household or her other guests. Don't forget to always clean up after him so that guests won't step in any unwanted surprises.

Accepting an invitation with your pet can be great fun, but it is also a great responsibility. Even the most well-mannered dog can become poorly behaved in a new environment. If at any time your dog becomes a serious problem, be prepared to leave immediately, or arrange for suitable care at a nearby facility. Also, be prepared to replace or repair any items that your dog destroys while at your host's home. If you carefully supervise your pet, bring the appropriate equipment, and can deal with the

unexpected—all while mingling with friends or family—
then you can both enjoy your time away from home.
Always remember, within a week of departing her home,
send your host a thank-you note. Let her know that it
was kind of her to include your dog, and that you both
had a great time.

PRODUCT RESOURCE GUIDE

Before leaving home, don't forget to bring
a gift for the host. Since you will spend
time together eating and drinking, take her a bottle of
wine from the Mutt Lynch Winery, located in Sonoma
County, California. She will be amused by the choices
of Merlot Over and Play Dead, Portrait Of A Mutt Zin-
fandel, Canis Major Syrah, or Unleashed Chardonnay
(*www.muttlynchwinery.com*).

Travel to a friend's house with a portable, soft kennel
by Petgear (*www.petgearinc.com*).

The Urine-Off Travel Kit allows you to use a black light
to locate stains that you can't see. Then you can treat
the soiled area with Urine-Off stain and odor eliminator
(*www.urineoff.com*).

Use elegant pet stationery to write your host a thank-
you note (*www.the-petset.com*).

Chapter 21

TRAVELING WITH CANINE *Panache*

If she likes adventure, is well-behaved, and can remain calm when left alone in a friendly, but foreign, environment, then (and only then!) your dog is ready to take a vacation or a business trip with you. Although many pet owners do not realize it, traveling with our dogs is a privilege not to be taken lightly. You are pet ambassadors wherever you go, so act accordingly. Promote good "dog" will.

Believe it or not, there are folks who dislike pets! Plus, of course, there are people who are allergic to animals. So we must practice our pet etiquette by being considerate to our fellow travelers when we are traveling by plane or automobile or staying at a hotel.

FLYING THE DOG-FRIENDLY SKIES

Over the years, major airlines such as American, Continental, Delta, and United have enhanced their animal-acceptance policy to transport pets as more than just cargo. These airlines allow passengers to carry on pets in soft-sided carriers that are small enough to stow beneath the seat directly in front of them. However, they also require that pets stay in those carriers for the duration of the flight. Additionally, to reduce stress and potential problems for both two-legged and four-legged travelers, airline policies stipulate that pets must remain in their carry bags while in the boarding area and airport lounges, and during

PET TIP

Prior to leaving your home, take her travel blanket or carrier liner and put it in your dirty clothes hamper for a few days. This will ensure that your scent remains on the item, keeping her cozy for the long trip ahead.

boarding or disembarking from the plane. For more information, always check with your airline for its specific pet regulations.

Before traveling, purchase a travel carrier that is big enough for your dog to turn around in and lie down. You should let her get accustomed to the carrier well before your trip and ensure that she can comfortably relax with her favorite blanket and toy. You don't want her crying and whining to get out, disturbing other passengers while in flight. If necessary, seek the advice of a dog trainer to help you acclimate your pet to the travel bag. Also take precautionary measures to prevent her from having an accident while traveling. Feed and water her after you arrive at your destination, or, if you and your pet companion are traveling for more than a few hours, give her a few biscuits and an ice cube to prevent her from being hungry or thirsty. Don't forget to let your dog exercise and eliminate just moments before putting her in the travel bag upon entering the airport.

If your dog does have an accident, be prepared. When traveling, I carry a small plastic bag, a hand towel, and pet wipes in the larger pocket of my pet travel bag. If my dog has an accident in his travel bag, I clean him and his bag only in the plane or terminal bathrooms. After wiping off the dog, I remove the waste from the travel bag. If I can, I spot-clean the liner so it will not smell, put it in the plastic bag, and place it in the larger pocket of the travel bag. Next, I wash out the inside of the travel bag, replace the liner with a hand towel, and put the dog back in the bag.

TIPS ON TRAVELING WITH A DOG AND DEALING WITH AIRPORT PERSONNEL

These days airline travel can be extremely stressful, especially with changing regulations, the long lines of disenchanted travelers, and possible delays. With a dog along for the ride, this stress can reduce any person to a tearful downpour. But if you have a clear understanding of the requirements and nuances of travel with poochie, you will be prepared to deal with airline personnel and airport employees in any situation.

Generally, when you fly your pet in cargo or as checked baggage, you don't have as much interaction with airport personnel. But when you fly with your dog in tow, you interface with airlines and airport employees throughout your trip.

Well in advance of leaving home, check with the airline to confirm your pooch's reservation, all airline procedures, and federal regulations. The night before traveling, don't forget to pack her health travel certificate, dated seven to ten days before traveling.

On the day of travel, even if you have only carry-on luggage, arrive at the airport at least two hours prior to the flight, because you will still need to wait in line and buy your dog a ticket. And yes, even if your dog is flying under the seat, you have to buy her a ticket. While the charge for a dog flying cargo depends on the size of his kennel and the total weight, the ticket price for a dog flying with you, under the seat, is approximately $80 to $100 dollars.

Remember, as a carry-on your dog will take the place of one carry-on bag. So be sure to consolidate all of your luggage in order to comply with the luggage requirements. When you reach the ticket counter, be prepared to hand over your identification, her health certificate,

PET TIP

When taking any trip with your pet, always bring the following:

❊ Pet identification tags that list your name and telephone numbers.

❊ A current picture to make into a poster in the event you and your pet are accidentally separated.

❊ A first-aid kit with your vet's business card, your pet insurance information, the ASPCA Poison Control Number (1-888-426-4435), a current health certificate, and a list of her medications.

and your credit card in order to claim your boarding pass and buy her a ticket. Don't be surprised if the ticket agent wants to get a sneak peak. Federal rules and regulations insist that dogs be at least eight weeks of age to travel and appear to be in good physical health.

When the representative hands you the receipt for your purchase of your dog's ticket, immediately put it with your boarding pass, because you will need to show both of these to the security and gate representatives. Moreover, some airlines require that your travel bag be tagged, signifying that you are traveling with a companion pet. Before you walk away from the counter, ask the representative if you need a travel tag for your pet carrier. If you do, put the tag on the bag before leaving the counter.

Next stop, airport security. When you reach the security checkpoint area, if they recognize that you are carrying a dog carrier, airport personnel will sometimes ask to see the receipt for her flight. Don't balk; show it to them so that you can move on quickly.

Although both of you will endure the long security lines, you have the burden of carrying her additional pounds. Because of this, many seasoned pet travelers prefer wheeled pet carriers in which they pack very little other than their dog. Depending on current regulations, you may be able to either carry on or buy a bottle of water in the airport. Don't forget to pack her portable water bowl for a tidy drinking experience.

When you finally get to the screeners, take her out of her bag just before it is to go through the x-ray machine. Take her collar off and put it in her travel bag, because the collar may cause the machine to go off, forcing you to go through the machine two or three more times. When walking through the x-ray machine, move slowly. Although the airport security personnel seem serious and at times rather difficult, the one thing that does often make them smile is a dog. Even though you might be tired and grumpy, answer their questions and accept their compliments politely. Just do it all while continuing through the security procedures, because you don't want to incur the wrath of the travelers behind you in line.

When you finally arrive at your gate, avoid security confrontations of all kinds by keeping your dog in her travel bag. If you need to give her water or pet her for comfort, do it all while she is confined in the carrier. Because of regular airport delays, I travel with a portable pop-up tent that can easily be folded up in your purse or briefcase but is big enough for her to move around in. With layovers, this can be a godsend.

To avoid delays boarding the plane, show your boarding pass and her ticket purchase receipt to the gate representative. And, even in flight, keep her in her carrier, because you don't want to get a scolding from a flight attendant.

LAYOVER BUDDIES

Once while traveling from Atlanta, I got stuck at the airport with a three-hour delay. While I was sitting outside my gate, a woman noticed my dog carrier, came over, introduced herself, and asked to see my dog, Thames. Although I did not take him out of the carrier, I opened it up so she could admire and pet him. She liked Thames so much that she asked her three friends to come over and see him, too. After a few minutes, we started conversing about dogs and everything else imaginable. Before she left for her flight, she told me that her daughter was very actively involved with dogs and showing. I gave her my card and told her to call or have her daughter call any time she would be in the New York area. A few weeks later, her daughter did call, because she was coming to New York for a dog show. We arranged to meet. When I got to the show, the daughter told me she had a surprise for me. Her mother had decided to come, meet us, and take us out for lunch. It just goes to show you, having a dog ensures that you will always meet new friends.

DOGGY ROAD TRIP

Although plane travel is popular for dogs and their owners, according to the Travel Industry Association road trips are even more widely enjoyed. Nearly eight in ten travelers (76 percent) take a road trip with Fido in an automobile, a truck, or a recreational vehicle.

Even though you may be tempted to have her ride shotgun in the passenger seat or roam loose about the cabin while you are driving, think twice. Canine car equipment, such as crates, car seats, and safety belts, keeps driving distractions to a minimum and helps avoid human and pet injuries in the event of an accident or an unexpected bump in the road.

MISS FIDO MANNERS ON . . .
Favorite Places to Go with Her Dogs

Aspen, CO: Stay at Little Nell's, where your dog will enjoy the scrumptious pet menu and brush up on hotel etiquette with their doggy primer.

Atlanta, GA: Meet other dog owners at Piedmont Park.

Austin, TX: Let your dog go swimming in Bull Creek.

Chicago, IL: Enjoy the White Sox's Dog Day Game, the oldest Major League Baseball team to invite dogs.

Denver, CO: Visit with dog Lily Prentiss at Hotel Monaco.

Knoxville, TN: Pitstop at PetSafe's Village and Public Dog Park.

Los Angeles, CA: Go to any of the animal charity events and see dogs and their pet-owning stars on the red carpet.

Miami, FL: Two-legged and four-legged guests can eat together on the patio overlooking the pool at South Beach's Loews Hotel.

New York, NY: View the runway show at Pet Fashion Week.

Scottsdale, AZ: Shop at Mackie's Dog Parlour, A Boutique for Dogs.

San Diego, CA: Attend one of the W Hotel's legendary "Yappy Hours."

San Francisco, CA: Walk your dog over the Golden Gate Bridge.

Seattle, WA: Ride one of the state ferries.

Toronto, Ontario: Go to Woofstock, the largest outdoor dog festival in North America and don't forget to stop by the Le Royal Meriden's King Edward Hotel and order the doggy tea service.

To keep your pet at ease, stop every two or three hours to allow her to eliminate, drink water, and get some exercise. Leash her securely before she exits the car; an unleashed pet, no matter how well trained, could frighten other travelers, become overwhelmed by her unfamiliar surroundings and bolt away, or even get hit by another vehicle.

Many rest stops have dog areas, a place where your dog can get some exercise and eliminate. Remember to be considerate to other dog owners and clean up after your pet. Also, it's best not to leave your pet alone in a car, as she could be stolen, experience severe weather conditions, or suffer from the anxiety of being deserted in a strange place.

HOTEL STAYS

When you arrive at a hotel, create a favorable impression by arriving with a clean dog who is flea- and tick-free. Hopefully you have arrived at a location that is pet-friendly. Finding what seems to be an appropriate place for both of you is not enough; call and confirm that the hotel's idea of pet-friendly is the same as yours. Pet rules and regulations frequently change, and travel guides on the market and vacation brochures can be outdated as soon as they are published. Before making your reservation, ask questions about the size and number of pets allowed, whether there are any additional pet fees or deposits that they may charge or waivers that need to be signed, and what their policy is about pets being left alone in the room. Also, discuss the areas of the hotel in which pets are allowed and other special accommodations or pet perks they offer.

RESIDENT DOGS

At a few hotels, one of the pet perks is having a resident house dog on the staff. These dogs work on the premises every day, greeting guests and spreading good cheer. Before there was Denver's Lily Prentiss, Boston's

Kate Copley, and Atlanta's Indie Indigo, there was New York City's Sophie Knorr. I met Sophie while she was living with her mother, the general manager of a grand midtown hotel. Sophie eventually moved out to the West Coast and became the grande dame of a very fashionable San Francisco hotel. Once in San Francisco, she was older and wasn't seen as much, preferring to spend her days quietly under her mother's desk, avoiding guests at all costs.

There is a certain cachet in staying at a hotel with a live-in dog. But, please, when you do, be considerate of the dog and her owner. Although you and your pet may love dogs, don't annoy the resident house dog. The biggest complaint of hotel pet parents is that clients want to "treat" their dogs well all day long, even when there is a sign that says "Please don't feed the dog." Hotel dogs need to stay slim and trim and have energy to meet and greet all hotel guests. Instead of treats, give the house dog a good rubdown—but only if she grants you permission. Those of you with children should allow them to visit with the resident dog for a short period of time, but only under your constant supervision to guarantee that your children and the dog will treat each other respectfully. And travelers with dogs shouldn't expect the resident dog to be a constant companion to your dog. Like people, some dogs just don't hit it off. Also, recognize that hotel dogs don't always want to play or be social;

they need some downtime, too. So, if you see the hotel dog resting under a lobby chair or sofa, leave her alone and let her have some peace and quiet.

MAKING HOTEL STAYS FUN AND EASY

Keeping your dog engaged with outdoor activities, like sightseeing and playing with other dogs at a nearby park, will calm and relax her once she needs to be indoors. Other than burning off her excess energy, it is important to keep her as comfortable as possible in her new environment by maintaining her routine. Pack her food, treats, bowls, and toys that she's accustomed to playing with, and try to have the same ratio of quiet to playtime as she would in an average day. Arrange to have the staff clean your room while you and your dog are gone so that there are no surprises or disruptions to frighten her.

Occasionally, the change of surroundings alone may be enough to agitate even the best-mannered dog, making her become ill-mannered and destructive. If you think she might become a nervous chewer, plan ahead. Bring or borrow a crate from your hotel, or confine her to the bathroom with a puppy gate. If she's a barker, you'll have to either spend every minute of the day with her or hire a hotel-recommended pet nanny to keep her company while you are out.

To make cleaning up on a daily basis as easy as possible for yourself and the housekeeping staff, feed your pooch in the bathroom so you can wipe up food crumbs or slobber from the tile floor. If she likes to sleep in bed with you, bring an extra sheet or blanket to prevent shedding or soiling. If she has an accident, pack an odor and stain remover to clean the carpet. More importantly, when you check out, make sure you leave your room the way you found it when you arrived—intact!

PRODUCT RESOURCE GUIDE

Thinking about where to travel to with your pet? Purchase *Fido Friendly* magazine and find out the best places to vacation with your dog (*www.fidofriendly.com*).

When traveling with your dog, use a Sherpa soft-sided carrier (*www.sherpapet.com*), a Petmate Kennel (*www.petmate.com*), or an Auto Cruiser Car Seat at *www.midnightpass.com*.

To keep your pet calm while traveling or when in the hotel room, use Comfort Zone with D.A.P. (Dog Appeasing Pheromones), a product that mimics natural calming pheromones and helps reduce stress. The product comes in two forms: a wall plug-in or a spray bottle.

Carry your pet's health certificate and related medical papers in the Ruffwear K-9 First-Aid Kit (*www.ruffwear .com*).

Traveling with Your Pet: The AAA Pet Book helps make your trip as easy as possible. This book, available at various AAA locations and bookstores, lists more than 10,000 pet-friendly accommodations throughout the United States and Canada; highlights pet-friendly places; includes a directory of airlines, animal hospitals, and other pet-related organizations; and offers pet travel tips. Visit *www.aaa.com*.

Chapter 22

BEACH DOG *Behavior*

Surf's up, but not always for your sand- and sea-loving pooch! In recent years, dog access to beaches has been curtailed because dog owners have disregarded public laws and have created nuisances with their pets. The beaches that still allow dogs should be treasured and cared for like rare jewels.

WHERE AND WHEN TO HAVE FUN IN THE SUN

Before heading down to the ocean with your pup for fun and sun, check with the municipal or state park authorities to determine whether your dog is allowed on the beach, as dogs are forbidden on the beaches or boardwalks in most seaside communities. The diminishing numbers of communities that do allow dogs have dog restrictions pertaining to the month of the year, time of day, on/off leash status and type, and designated play areas.

If your dog is allowed on the beach, it is almost certainly not during tourist season. By and large, dog bans are enacted from the beginning of May until the end of September. If your dog is permitted on public beaches during these months, he is usually accepted in the morning hours up until 9:00 A.M. or after 6:00 P.M., avoiding times in which the bathing area is heavily populated with family beachgoers and sun-worshipers.

BEACH LEASH LAWS

No matter what time of the year, and even if your dog is allowed on the sand, please comply with the leash laws. One factor that has limited or restricted dog access to the seashore is owners who have disregarded these laws, allowing their dog to roam free and disturb beach-goers, other dogs and their owners, and even public officials. An off-leash dog—no matter how friendly—can frighten those enjoying their day at the beach, or potentially get into a seaside row with another dog, causing dogs, their owners, and others to get injured. Some leash rules are so particular that they include restrictions about the lengths of leads that dog owners can use. When leash lengths are mentioned, usually either six- or eight-foot leads are deemed appropriate, and your dog should never be frolicking at the end of a long training lead or a retractable leash.

Arnold, Lori's German shorthaired pointer, is a good example of the importance of leashes at the beach. Arnold was fond of playing in the sand, but he was not enthusiastic about coming when called. Once while walking with her on the beach, he stopped, sniffed, and took off. Although Lori couldn't catch him, she saw that his destination

PET TIP

To prevent skin irritations, always rinse your dog with warm water after he comes home from the beach.

was a house adjacent to the beach, and as she sprinted toward the home, she saw her dog run inside. She cautiously approached the open glass doors of the home to retrieve her pet, and witnessed the homeowner catching her dog eating chicken off a plate on the dining room table. Fortunately, the homeowner (and dog lover) found the incident rather amusing. Now, when you see Lori on the beach, Arnold is always on a leash.

ENVIRONMENTAL CONCERNS

Another reason that dog admission has been curbed oceanside is that dog owners were not picking up dog waste, which contains disease-carrying bacteria that can make adults and children ill. In some cases, dog waste has polluted the ocean, resulting in the closing of beaches and the banning of bathers from the area waters. So, if your dog is permitted to spend some time having fun on the beach, please scoop the poop. By doing so, you are being kind to our environment, too! Poop isn't the only way that your pooch can harm the beach environment: wandering dogs can disturb nests and destroy plant life that grows on coastal shores. In many cases, birds will not return to their nests if they have been disturbed.

DOG BEACH

To make conciliatory measures for dog owners, some local governments and state parks have designated shore-line dog play areas. Think of a "dog beach" as you would a "dog park." While at the dog beach, always supervise and clean up after your dog. Practice your recall command so that you can have verbal control over him when he is off-leash. And, because many people like to play fetch with their dogs by throwing a ball into the ocean and having him swim out to retrieve it, play it safe by having him wear a life vest while he is in the water.

Just as many grains of sand contribute to a beach, you, as a dog owner, can abide by the dog regulations to help preserve continued use and enjoyment of the seaside by all dog-lovers and their four-legged friends.

MISS FIDO MANNERS ON . . .
Ruff Surfing

How fun would it be to "hang ten" with your best friend? Vacation at The Loews Coronado Bay Resort and Spa in Coronado, California, and take dog surfing lessons at the Coronado Surfing Academy on Coronado's dog beach. The guest package includes accommodations, a copy of *The Dog's Guide to Surfing,* an owner's manual for hanging ten with man's best friend, a surf 'n'turf dog supper, and more.

PRODUCT RESOURCE GUIDE

To research dog-friendly beaches and their rules, visit *www.petfriendly.com.*

Once you are seaside, protect your dog from the sun by applying Pet Screen with an SPF of 15 to his skin and coat (*www.doggles.com*).

If you have a dog who loves to swim, ensure his safety by having him wear a Float Coat, which is highly visible and has a reflective trim, by *www.ruffwear.com.*

If he likes a good game of water fetch, use the Planet Dog Orbee, which floats in the ocean. Visit *www.planet dog.com*.

After a water workout, dry him off with a Soggy Dog Towel (*www.farfetchedinc.com*). Put your hands in the towel pockets to rub him down and get the sand out of his coat.

End the day with a special treat, some doggy ice-cream by Dogsters (*www.dogateers.com*).

Chapter 23

Happy TRAILS

Those of you who enjoy the exhilarating experience of the great outdoors—share it with your dog! Take her hiking, but while out in nature with your dog, engage in "minimal-impact" hiking. This outdoor philosophy means that a good hiker with his companion dog abides by park rules, does not pollute the environment, stays on the required trails, keeps noise to a minimum, and protects vegetation. By doing so, you will inflict minimal harm to flora and fauna while enjoying your trek.

TREKKING IN STATE PARKS

In response to the growing trend of pet owners who like to hike with their pets, more national and state parks welcome domesticated animals. Still, before traveling, check the national or state park Web sites or telephone the parks department for dog-particular information. Thus you will ensure that your trip is agreeable and not dog-burdensome.

In most parks, pets are not permitted on beaches and playgrounds, or in bathing areas, cabins, park buildings, and concession facilities. At some locations, dogs are allowed in the campgrounds, but not on the hiking trails, or they have limited access to the paved trails and the back country.

Jonathan was exposed to one danger of hiking with his dog when he decided to take him for a day hike with a local San Francisco singles group. He hopped a ride to the state park with a friend and his dog. While on the trail, he let his foxhound nose around in a hollow log. Within a few minutes, Jonathan's foxhound and the dog that was standing next to him were "skunked." Rachel, the owner of the other skunked dog, led Jonathan back down the trail to deal with the problem. She was a regular on these day hikes, so she knew to pack an odor eliminator product in her

PET TIP

When buying a pack for your dog, choose one that is brightly colored with reflective trim, is waterproof, and places the bags over the dog's shoulders. Avoid packs that extend down the length of a dog's back, as they may cause a back injury. Fit the pack snugly so that only two fingers fit between the dog and the equipment.

Jeep. Rachel told Jonathan that they should forget about spending the day with the rest of the group, and should take their stinky dogs back to the city. She said that the three-hour drive would give the de-skunking product a few hours to saturate the dogs' coats and skin, and by the time they got home, the animals would be ready for a good bath. During the ride home, the dog owners found that they had a lot in common, continued the conversation through bathing the dogs at Rachel's house, and over dinner at a nearby restaurant. Since their "first date," Jonathan and Rachel have been inseparable and are now engaged.

PLANNING AND PREPPING FOR YOUR HIKE

Before heading out, plan a hike that your pet can manage comfortably and make sure she is in optimal condition so that you can both enjoy your trip. Prior to an outdoor adventure, you can build up your pet's stamina by engaging in frequent and progressively longer distance walks each day. If she is going to be wearing gear on the hike, such as a backpack and boots, have her walk in the equipment weeks before, starting with one item and gradually adding on the rest of the equipment that she will be carrying on the trip. What she carries should never weigh more than a quarter of her body weight and should include fresh drinking water, water bowl, and a pet first-aid kit. Don't just carry a pet first-aid kit, though; be familiar with the contents and know how to use the supplies to wrap leg injuries, deal with poisonous plants such as poison ivy, or extract nettles. Also, check that your nature-loving dog is up-to-date with all vaccinations, including rabies, because many state and national parks will require you to show proof of this for admittance. Don't forget to bring a copy of her health certificate along with you.

APPROPRIATE PARK BEHAVIOR

While at the park, your pooch should be quiet, well-behaved, and under your control at all times. She should be attached to you by a six-foot lead and never tied to a tree, bush, table, or any of the park facility buildings. With so many scent distractions, it might be difficult for a dog like a beagle to be on its best behavior. But keep in mind that pets that are noisy, destructive to wildlife, or intimidating to other dogs or hikers will not be tolerated, and you will be asked to leave the park grounds with your dog immediately. Dogs are also prohibited from romping in the springs so as to prevent them from urinating and polluting the water supply for wild animals. As always, clean up after your pet and follow the park's procedures for disposing of the fecal waste, which may include burying it.

While with your companion animal at a state or a national park, be considerate of park staff, hikers, campers, and their dogs, and treat wildlife with care and respect. By doing so, you will help guarantee that a great outdoor experience can be shared by other dogs and their owners.

MISS FIDO MANNERS ON . . .
Field Trips

If you like the outdoor life, take a hiking or canoeing day trip with your dog. These guided tours give you the opportunity to socialize with a pack of fellow dog lovers and have fun in nature. Although the participants on most of these field trips are big dogs, small dog owners should never be intimidated, because you can always carry your dog in a doggy backpack. Try one of the great trips conducted by Canada's Dog Paddling Adventures (*www.dogpaddlingadventures .com*).

Also, Loews Denver Hotel offers The Outward Hound package for vacationers and their pampered pets. Two-legged and four-legged guests receive pet-related amenities, such as a pet travel bag with water bowl, a map of pet-friendly trails, and more. If you are gone for the day, arrange a personal pet hike for your dog with the hotel staff. (*www.loewshotels.com*)

PRODUCT RESOURCE GUIDE

For a list of the national parks that admit dogs, purchase *Traveling with Your Pet: The AAA Pet Book* at *www.aaa.com* or visit *www.dog friendly.com* for information about hiking in state and national parks.

For outdoor gear including packs, boots, leashes, jackets, and other supplies, browse *www.granitegear .com*.

Don't leave home without a lightweight first-aid kit. Visit *www.ruffwear.com*.

Be prepared if your dog gets skunked; bring Sea-Yu's Skunk Odor Eliminator and Cleaner to remove skunk odors from dogs, people, and affected surfaces. Visit *www.sea-yu.com*.

Chapter 24

BEING A *Good Sport* AT THE BALLPARK

What's the latest pet trend for dogs and their owners? Sharing their favorite activities with each other. One of the more popular activities that two- and four-legged best friends can share is attending baseball games.

More than a decade ago, the Chicago White Sox had their first Dog Day promotion. White Sox fans of all ages brought their dogs to the ballpark to enjoy the game. Since then, other Major League Baseball teams have opened their gates to baseball enthusiasts and their canine companions. At the inception, these promotions consisted of pets and their owners sitting in a designated section of the bleachers to watch the game, but now these "Bark at the Park" games have evolved into big events, with as many as 500 dogs attending the game and the pre-game activities.

PROPER PRE-GAMING

Pre-game activities are organized as tailwag parties in which dogs and their owners can participate in costume contests, have their picture taken with locker room backdrops or retired ball players, cool off in wading pools and overhead showers, learn basic agility, and compete in other doggy games. The highlight of these pre-game activities, if you are lucky, is the parade of dogs and their owners walking around the warming track.

While at the game, participants also have the opportunity to learn about pet services offered by pet professionals in their area; buy pet supplies and other dog-related products from local vendors; visit with nearby animal shelters that raise awareness about pet adoption; and go home with doggy goodie bags supplied by game sponsors, such as Central Garden & Pet, Del Monte, Hill's Science Diet, Iams, and Purina. Veterinarians are present to deal with emergencies, especially heatstroke.

DRESSING FOR THE OCCASION

In recent years, many of the major league ball clubs have been concerned with the appearance of their players. In 2006, some Chicago White Sox players were asked by the team's owner to get haircuts to look more presentable. Similarly, to make your dog feel as comfortable as possible and look the part of an MVP (most venerated pooch), have him come to the game clean and well-groomed. And, just like the players, have your coifed dog wear an officially licensed, pet-safe jersey or jacket, accessorized with leash and collar.

HOW TO KEEP THE DAY SAFE AND FUN

If you are interested in attending a game with your pet, check to see if your local major, or even minor, league team has a "dog day." You will need to buy a ticket for yourself and your dog and submit a waiver attesting that your dog is in good health and has complete and current vaccinations. Additionally, dogs must wear current rabies tags to be admitted to the ballparks.

Once, while at a St. Louis Cardinals game, I met a woman and her yellow Labrador sitting on the sidewalk, waiting patiently for the tailwag party to begin. When I asked her about her expectations of the "Purina Pooches in the Park" game, she told me that she wouldn't be attending the game because the tickets were sold out before she had the opportunity to buy one. However, she decided to come to the tailwag anyway because she wanted to take advantage of meeting other dog owners and participate in the pre-game activities with her dog.

PET TIP

Bring a small towel that you can wet to wipe your dog down if he gets overheated.

211

MISS FIDO MANNERS ON . . .

Other Events That You Can Enjoy with Your Pet

Doggy high teas: When given the opportunity to take high tea with my pooch, I am thrilled and RSVP immediately. Enjoy an afternoon with well-mannered, reserved, and well-groomed pooches. At these events, dogs are usually served some type of chicken or beef broth as tea, doggy spam sandwiches, savory scones, and yogurt-decorated cookies.

Pet art auctions: Meet an eclectic selection of dogs and their owners and enjoy the painting, drawing, photography, and sculpture of great subject matter—man's best friend. And if you bid on a piece of artwork, your money will help an animal shelter or rescue organization. At this type of event, dogs are kept on leashes and are expected to stroll around the exhibition with their owners.

Pet fashion shows: Just like celebrities, you and your dog should expect red-carpet attention and anticipate being photographed. Wear the latest fashions, and dress your dog in the most current doggy styles with a coordinating pet tote, leash, collar, and jewelry.

During the show, your dog will be expected to sit on your lap, or eye the runway from the floor, and be quiet as the dogs on the catwalk strut on by.

Yappy hours: At these festive events, pet owners generally drink wine; for pooches, the water is flowing and the treats are abundant. Dress your pet in fun party clothing, like doggy boas, snazzy T-shirts, costumes, or party dresses. A hint for eligible bachelors: these events are often full of beautiful, bright, single women.

When you come to the ballpark, bring a healthy and parasite-free dog. With so many dogs in attendance, you do not want to compromise the health of the other dogs at the event. At the game there are water stations so that your dog can take a drink to keep cool; but recognize that having your dog drink from a common water bowl could put him at risk for a communicable disease, such as kennel cough, or a microscopic parasite, such as *Giardia*. As a health measure, bring your own water bowl and buy him a bottle of water at the game.

With so many dogs present, sharing common potty areas can also spread fecal parasites. Make certain that your dog has taken his monthly heartworm medication, which helps control hookworms, roundworms, and whipworms. Instead of using the communal doggy bathroom, you might prefer having him eliminate right before entering and immediately after leaving the stadium. But wherever he poops, clean up the waste and dispose of it in appropriate trash receptacles. Also, with dogs in such proximity to each other, it is a good idea to give him his flea and tick control topical a few days before the game.

To avoid additional stress on such a long day, leave his toys at home and refrain from feeding him snacks in close proximity of other dogs. Breaking up dog fights in the stands can lead to potential disagreements with other pet owners and can only hinder a day of fun.

It is best to bring your dog only if he has a good temperament, is reliable in crowds, and is used to being around a lot of other dogs. Dogs that are aggressive, hyper, or have difficulty walking on a leash are not great companions to take to the ballgame. And if you have an exceptionally large dog, consider buying him an additional seat so that he can be as comfortable as possible and not in such propinquity to a dog or person that he does not know.

GAME ON

If you are given the opportunity, participate in the dog parade by walking around the warming track with pet owners and their dogs. At one San Francisco Giants game there were so many dogs in attendance that it took at least 40 minutes for all of them to walk around the field. Believe me, this is the real highlight of a dog game, but take care to not step on the grass. You might not realize it, but maintaining the grass at the ballpark takes a large staff, many hours of care, and a lot of money. If your dog needs to eliminate during the parade, keep him on the clay and clean up as much of the waste as possible.

The idea of attending a dog day game is to have fun with your dog, so before buying your ticket, determine whether the stadium conditions and his personality will contribute to both of you having a good time. If they do, sit back, relax, and watch the pros PLAY BALL!

PRODUCT RESOURCE GUIDE

Why stay home and watch the ballgame on television when you can take your dog to the ballpark? The following Major League Baseball teams have dog day games to which you can take your dog. Check their Web sites during baseball season for specific details.

Atlanta Braves: *www.atlantabraves.com*
Chicago White Sox: *www.whitesox.com*
Colorado Rockies: *www.coloradorockies.com*
Florida Marlins: *www.floridamarlins.com*

New York Mets: *www.mets.com*
Oakland Athletics: *www.oaklandathletics.com*
Pittsburgh Pirates: *www.pirates.com*
San Diego Padres: *www.padres.com*
San Francisco Giants: *www.sfgiants.com*
St. Louis Cardinals: *www.stlcardinals.com*
Texas Rangers: *www.texasrangers.com*

If you are looking for officially licensed team jerseys, jackets, leashes, and collars, visit *www.huntermfg .com* or *www.sportyk9.com*.

PART VI

Graciousness in the Worst of Times

Chapter 25

DOGS, CUSTODY, *and* DIVORCE

These days, it is not uncommon for us to treat our dogs like kids, or rather think of them as four-legged kids. Unfortunately, just like children of divorcing parents, dogs can become the subject of custody issues. If you are thinking about a divorce or are in the process of one, take the time to consider what is best for your dog.

PET PRENUPS

Over the last few years, the national media has reported on an increasing number of doggy divorce dramas. In fact, a 2006 poll of the American Academy of Matrimonial Lawyers membership noted that 90 percent of the member respondents answered that dogs are the most common animal caught in the middle of a divorce dispute. As a result of statistics like these and other findings, divorce lawyers, dog trainers, and other animal experts, including myself, have cautioned couples that they should think of their dog's future very early on in their relationship. Although it might be an uncomfortable topic, decide who gets the dog in a prenuptial agreement or other contract. It is better to do this when you first get the dog and can agree amicably, rather than later when you and your spouse or partner are in a contentious dispute and working out the decision may cost you upwards of thousands of dollars in legal fees. Other than your pocketbook, there is, of course, the effect of the divorce or separation on your pooch.

EASING SEPARATION ANXIETY

Dogs are social creatures who instinctively enjoy being part of a structured pack; to domesticated dogs, their human family is their pack. For dogs, family life is composed of a schedule of activities that makes sense to them based on the hierarchy of their pack (for example, the same person takes them for walks or feeds them at the same time every day). When that life is disturbed by divorce, dogs can suffer from anxiety and other maladies. If your dog is feeling the pressure of your breakup, she could "act out" or engage in bad behavior. Barking, crying, chewing, house-soiling, or what appears to be depression can be common responses for stressed dogs experiencing the woes of divorcing pet parents.

If your dog is showing signs of uneasiness about the current situation, try to reassure her by spending as much time with her as you can, while keeping her on her regular schedule. Studies from New York, the United Kingdom, and Germany have shown that spending time with dogs can be healthy for and therapeutic to humans, so by taking some extra time walking and petting her, you and your baby can both relax.

Although you may consider her practically human, the courts still consider dogs to be chattel, or property. If you were the one who brought the dog into the relationship, she will probably exit with you as your personal property. But if the court determines that your dog is marital property, she may be awarded to the spouse with a closer relationship or the pet parent who is the better doggy caregiver—both of which can be subjective and cause for contention.

CUSTODY WOES

If you are getting divorced, don't be embarrassed to tell your lawyer how much your pet means to you. Tell him either you want custody of your dog or will settle for visitation rights. If your lawyer has no experience with pet custody issues, suggest that he seek advice from an animal lawyer with pet custody experience who can help the two of you work out this problem—under your lawyer's supervision, of course. Once you and your ex determine where the dog will live, and whether there will be any visitation specifics, then discuss the cost of the veterinary care, grooming, and training, or other services needed and costs necessary to maintain your pet.

In some families, there will be other factors. If you have children, it is probably best that the dogs and the kids stay together, especially in a house that has younger children. Kids often talk to their pets like they do to dolls or stuffed animals. Dogs can serve as confidantes for children, and they might need to share their thoughts about the divorce with their four-legged "siblings."

PET TIP

If you and your spouse are having real trouble at home, or if it is time for one of you to move out, send the dog to a boarding kennel for a week or two, at least until things settle down.

Another situation that can be difficult to deal with is when more than one pet is involved. Some couples want to split up their dogs, thinking that at least they'll each have one (kind of like the movie *The Parent Trap*). That doesn't work either. Dogs that have been together for a long time might become seriously depressed if separated because they can no longer enjoy each other's company while playing, eating, walking, and sleeping.

REMEMBER WHAT'S BEST FOR YOUR DOG
Like humans, dogs are sensitive creatures who can respond to changes in your home. If you are thinking about or are in the process of getting a divorce, you and your spouse should try to put your hostility aside and determine what is best for your pet. Whatever decision the two of you make, remember: your dog will always love both of you.

Amanda, a civil engineer, and Bruce, an investment banker, had to deal with doggy custody after being married for five years. They both worked very long hours, so when Amanda wanted to get a dog, Bruce thought she was not being realistic about the time they would have for such an addition. Once Amanda brought home Beatrice, a little mixed-breed terrier from the local animal shelter, Bruce fell in love with her. The two cared for Beatrice equally, walking her, feeding her, and playing with her. When the couple decided to split up, Amanda and Bruce thought it best that Beatrice live with Amanda and that Bruce would visit her on the weekends. A few years have passed, and Beatrice still lives with Amanda and her boyfriend, the owner of two cats. Beatrice stays with Bruce and his partner when Amanda goes on holiday; and when Bruce and his partner, also the owner of a dog, go on vacation, they send the other dog over to Amanda's to visit with Beatrice. How's that for modern family life!

PRODUCT RESOURCE GUIDE

Although you have to sign up and pay a small fee, *www.divorcesource.com* has some informative articles about divorce and pet custody. The articles discuss case law and why the courts ruled in favor or one pet parent over another.

Use the member directory of the American Academy of Matrimonial Lawyers (*www.aaml.org*) to find a divorce lawyer.

To learn more about pet custody issues in your state, contact your local city bar association. Many city bar associations have standing committees on legal issues pertaining to animals.

Chapter 26

The Etiquette OF
RELINQUISHING YOUR PET

Unfortunately, life's circumstances change, and there are times when some of us are confronted with the decision of whether to give up our pets. But before deciding to relinquish your pet, please investigate all possibilities for keeping him. If you really can't maintain him, take the time to find him a good home prior to leaving him with a local animal shelter.

TRY TO FIND A SOLUTION

If your decision to relinquish your pet is based on behavior, a pet illness, a landlord/tenant dispute regarding your pet, your having a baby, or a family member's pet allergies, there could be an easy solution to your problem. For pet owners who perceive their problem to be behavior-related, note that many animal shelters have help lines that troubled pet owners can call for free advice. As a preventive measure against pet surrenders, help line counselors offer the organization's dog-training classes at an extremely discounted price. If your pet is ill and you are worried about the high medical costs, consider calling your local SPCA, humane society, animal shelter, or a nearby veterinary school to seek out their veterinary services. Generally, at these facilities, pet owners receive veterinary care at significantly reduced fees. If you are worried about a landlord/tenant dispute that involves your dog, ask a local tenant group, councilman's office, or low-cost legal service group to assist you. These organizations have experience with this kind of problem, and they could offer some good advice.

If you are having a baby, don't fret. You have other options than dropping your dog off at the nearest animal shelter. Discuss how best to manage the new baby and your dog with your veterinarian. In many cases, your veterinarian can recommend books or can give you the name and number of a dog trainer who can help you prepare for your new human bundle of joy. I recommend *Child-Proofing Your Dog* by Brian Kilcommons and Sarah Wilson and *There's a Baby in the House: Preparing Your Dog for the Arrival of Your Child* by Mike Wombacher.

If you or someone living in your home has allergies, speak to your veterinarian about products that can reduce allergens on your pet and in your home, or speak to your doctor about prescription medication or injections that can help you. But sometimes if you are moving or have too many pets, re-homing your dog might be your only viable solution.

FINDING A NEW HOME

Before turning your pet over to any animal placement organization, try to find him a good home on your own. A good home is one in which he will be treated like a family member for the rest of his life and receive lots of love, quality veterinary care, a healthy diet, appropriate toys, adequate exercise, necessary grooming, and basic training. To start the re-homing process, create a one-sheet profile of your dog. Include two pictures (one showing his face and the other showing his body type) and any significant information, such as his age, size, breed, personality, and health. Discuss his likes and dislikes. Mention whether he prefers men or women. Let the reader know if he enjoys spending time with children or other pets. Most importantly, be truthful, because you want an interested individual to review your pet's profile and deem him a "good fit" with her lifestyle.

To discourage individuals who are not serious adopters, ask for a small adoption fee. I suggest that your adoption fee be one-twelfth of your dog's yearly expenses of food, veterinary care, grooming services, holiday care, and any other necessities. This way, if given the opportunity, you can discuss the financial obligation of taking care of your dog based on what one month of care will cost.

Your next step is to ask family members, friends, neighbors, work colleagues, dog lovers, and pet professionals (veterinarians, groomers, or pet sitters) if they would like to adopt a dog or know any one else who would. If they seem interested, give them his profile and ask them to call you when they have time to talk about your pet. If you do get any interest from a prospective new owner, you must screen her thoroughly and check out her home very carefully. Ask her if she understands how to care for a dog, the time commitment involved, and the financial responsibilities of having a dog. If at any time, you don't feel comfortable with her responses, consider another person or alternative option. Also, don't be shy or feel that it is impolite to ask to visit her home with your pet. Explain that you want to make certain that he will be properly taken care of and that he will adjust to his new environment. If any potential candidates prefer that you not visit their homes or meet their families, immediately eliminate them as re-homing possibilities.

The Andersons were a retired couple who had to give up their beloved Maggie, an American cocker spaniel, due to their move to an assisted living facility that did not permit dogs. Although approved to enter the facility, the couple would not move unless they could find a loving home for Maggie. Over a two-week period, they

PET TIP

When you relinquish your pet, send him with his favorite toy or blanket for comfort and a small bag of food to avoid stomach upset. Do not give all of his possessions to the shelter, because they cannot guarantee that they will stay with him.

spoke to, called, wrote, or visited everyone they knew in the hope of finding her a proper home. After he asked her why she looked so upset one day, Mrs. Anderson told the doorman of her apartment building the problem that she and her husband were having with finding Maggie a new home. The doorman was very fond of Maggie, but couldn't take her home because his wife was extremely allergic to dogs. But he had another idea. He knew of a tenant in the building who had recently lost her pet. He spoke to her about the Andersons' situation with Maggie, and the tenant agreed to consider meeting Maggie. After a few days of visiting Maggie, and then having Maggie come to her apartment, each time increasing the length of a visit until the two had a full sleep-over, she decided to adopt Maggie. Even though a few years have passed and Mr. Anderson has died, Mrs. Anderson still keeps in touch with Maggie's new family, sending Maggie toys and treats a few times a year, and Maggie's new mother always sends pictures.

Fortunately, with help, the Andersons found their dog Maggie a wonderful home. But if you have exhausted all of your personal and professional contacts, you will need to use a reputable organization and/or Web sites to help you. Don't make the mistake, as so many people have, of placing an advertisement in a newspaper offering your pet as "FREE to a good home." Unscrupulous people searching for laboratory animals, as well as dogfighters, obtain pets this way. If you do want to place an ad, consider a classified on an Internet adoption site managed by a rescue organization, like *www.petfinder.com*.

FINDING A SHELTER

Use *www.petfinder.com* if you need to find an animal shelter or rescue organization that can help you place your dog. When telephoning any animal shelter organization, the first question you should ask is "Are you a no-kill shelter?" This question is very important, because although the local animal control facilities or the city pound will adopt dogs to good homes, they also only tend to keep a dog about seventy-two hours before it is euthanized. Furthermore, when calling any rescue organization, ask about their relinquishment procedures and adoption policies. If you can, visit the facility to assure yourself that the animals are treated well, potential adopters are screened, and there is adoption support should problems arise with the dog.

When you are ready to relinquish your pet, you can either complete an application for relinquishment over the phone with an adoption counselor or download and complete the form on your own. The application will compromise a series of questions about his physique, history, health, habits, and behaviors. In cases where your dog has bitten a person or a child, there is a chance that you will need to complete a supplemental bite-disclosure form. In addition, you will need to submit proof of ownership or legal right to relinquish your pet. A kennel club registration form, a bill of sale for the dog, or your pet's medical record is sufficient evidence.

With most no-kill shelters, space is limited, so please do not expect your pet to be admitted the same day that you complete your application. It is very possible that a shelter representative will set an appointment for you to bring your pet at later date to have a health and behavior evaluation. This testing is necessary to determine whether your dog is suitable for adoption. Generally, your animal will have to pass both tests to be admitted into the shelter. If your dog does not pass the tests, some shelters might offer you euthanasia as a humane alternative. But even if your dog is admitted, you still might have to wait patiently until a space is available for him.

When the shelter does call for you to bring him in, you will probably have twenty-four hours to turn him over to the facility. Also, at the time of relinquishment, you will be required to pay a small fee. If the shelter does not require you to pay a fee, make a donation.

As heartbreaking as it is to relinquish a pet, please take the time to find a proper and quality home for your dog. It is worth the effort to ensure that he ends up in the best home possible with people who will love him for the rest of his life.

PRODUCT RESOURCE GUIDE

If you are looking to locate a shelter or rescue group, to learn how to take care of your pet, or to post a classified ad regarding re-homing your pet, start at *www.petfinder.com*. It is a Web site devoted to adoptable pets.

If you have a purebred dog and need to find him a home, visit *www.akc.org*. Check the Breed section of the Web site, and click on Breed Rescue to assist you with purebred rescue.

I recommend *Child-Proofing Your Dog* by Brian Kilcommons and Sarah Wilson (Warner Books, 1994) and *There's a Baby in the House: Preparing your Dog for the Arrival of Your Child* by Mike Wombacher (M. Wombacher, 2001).

Chapter 27

DEATH, BURIAL RITUALS, AND *Commemorative Services*

Saying goodbye to a beloved dog is not an easy task. You loved and cherished her as a member of your family, and in death you can still provide her with the dignity and respect that she deserves.

AN ACT OF MERCY

Although many dogs die naturally, some pet owners look to euthanasia as a humane act to end the suffering of their ill or seriously injured animal. This procedure involves administering a large dose of sodium pentobarbital to your dog, which causes her to fall into a deep sleep and, eventually, stop breathing. This final act of love can be performed at your home or in your vet's office. Talk to your veterinarian about what is best for you and your dog, and discuss what provisions can be made for the body after the procedure is over.

Making arrangements for your pet's remains is very similar to the provisions that you make for human loved ones. You can choose to bury your dog or have her cremated.

BURIAL AND CREMATION OPTIONS

Depending on where you live and your local health ordinances, you may be able to bury your pet on your own property. If allowed, a home burial allows you to keep your pet at home, close to you and other loved ones. If this option appeals to you, bury her in a non-biodegradable container in a deep grave to prevent a health hazard. In her honor, consider marking her grave with a memorial plaque, a bench, or a tree. If you bury her at home, a family memorial service can serve as a way for every member of the family, including other pets, to say goodbye.

For those who choose to cremate their dear pet, either you or your veterinarian can make the arrangements to have her body picked up at his office or at your home. Your dog can either be cremated with a group of other animals, or privately. In communal cremation, your pet's ashes can be returned to you, co-mingled with those of the other animals. With private cremation, your pet is cremated alone and only her ashes are returned to you. Once the ashes are returned, you can keep them in a decorative urn at home or at a pet cemetery. Another option is to sprinkle her ashes in the wind as a symbolic gesture of freedom of her spirit.

If you prefer to store her ashes or have cemetery burial, contact the International Association of Pet Cemeteries to learn about the standards of care and to obtain a list of pet cemeteries near you. The cost of pet burial depends on your choice of amenities (casket or vault, headstone, plaque, flowers, and maintenance). If you want a funeral service for your pet, let the cemetery staff help you with those arrangements. Generally, a pet pastor performs a nondenominational service, but you can incorporate elements of your own religion into the service, like a prayer or song, and other touches, like displaying a picture of your pet. Although the idea of a funeral might seem extravagant to some, many pet owners find this type of final tribute comforting.

PET TIP

At any time or at any age your pet could pass. Investigate all options early on to handle your pet's remains and your emotional needs.

PAYING HOMAGE

Besides having an official burial at a cemetery, a popular homage chosen by city dwellers is to have a memorial service at a dog park or dog run. If your dog was very popular and/or enjoyed socializing with her dog friends, invite dog owners for a Saturday or Sunday morning service. Speak to the local parks department or the dog-run supervising committee and ask to plant a tree in her honor or donate a bench with a remembrance plaque. Inform family, friends, or dog owners of your pet's passing by sending an email, mailing a note, or posting a doggy death notice on the bulletin board at the park. In the notice, include a picture of your dog, the date of her passing, and the date and time of the funeral service at the pet cemetery or memorial service at the dog park. It's okay to ask friends and family to make a donation to a breed club, veterinary school, local shelter, or dog park in your dog's memory, rather than sending flowers.

When Katie, an American cocker spaniel, was diagnosed with cancer, her owner, Roberta, decided to keep her as comfortable as possible. Eventually, euthanasia became the only humane option to end her suffering. When Katie died, Roberta asked her family and friends at the dog park to make donations to the College of Veterinary Medicine at Cornell University. Their generous donations exceeded her expectations.

If friends send flowers or make donations, acknowledge their expressions of sympathy by sending thank-you notes for their condolences and gifts.

Another means of informing people of your pet's death, and one that can help you feel better, is to write an obituary for your beloved dog. For a fee, you can place the obituary in a pet magazine or the newsletter of a local animal shelter or animal rescue organization.

GRIEVING FOR YOUR PET

While these ceremonial measures may help you celebrate and cherish your pet during this difficult time, make sure to give yourself time to grieve. If you need to talk about your feelings, share them with another pet owner or a therapist, or seek the support of a pet loss group. To find a therapist or support group, contact the Association of Pet Loss and Bereavement. This organization can provide you with the names of therapists, shelters, local humane societies, and veterinary schools that offer pet loss counseling.

MISS FIDO MANNERS ON . . .

Expressing Pet Condolences

There are many ways in which you can express your condolences to a family member or friend whose dog has died. One option is to send a sympathy card. Many card companies now offer pet sympathy cards, and you can find them in card, drug, or other stores in which cards are sold. If the owner of a deceased dog was interested in a particular pet charity, breed club, animal shelter, or rescue group, make a donation in memory of her pet.

Other persons and pets in your home may also be upset about the death of your dog. If you have children, provide them with simple and age-appropriate explanations regarding the death of your dog. Should your child seem anxious or have bad dreams, speak to his doctor about how best to handle the situation. Likewise, if other household pets seem depressed, try to comfort them with extra playtime, petting, or exercise.

To be confronted with the death of a beloved pet is an unpleasant experience. Make arrangements that you deem appropriate, but more importantly, take the time to grieve, because no one will be able to understand how much your companion animal meant to you or your family.

PRODUCT RESOURCE GUIDE

Contact the International Association of Pet Cemeteries to find a list of pet cemeteries near you and to review their standards (*www.iaopc.com*).

To seek support for your loss, contact the Association of Pet Loss and Bereavement at *www.aplb.org.*

Plant a tree as a living memorial to your best friend on public lands in any U.S. state (*www.treegivers.com*).

Or you can purchase a ready-to-plant cypress tree, the symbol of mourning, from *www.1800flowers.com*.

Place an obituary for your deceased pet in the *New York* or *Hollywood Dog* magazines (*www.thenydog.com* or *www.thehollywooddog.com*).

The Luxepets In Loving Memory Collection is designed to address the needs of a grieving pet owner with urns, remembrance cards, memorial candles, sympathy kits, and more (*www.luxepets.com*).

Epilogue

In recent years, dogs have become quite fashionable. The media reports their attendance at red carpet events; the luxury hotels in which they sojourn; their stylish clothing, fine jewelry and hi-tech toys; their access to plastic surgery and weight loss drugs; and even the amount money it costs to maintain them.

As a dog owner first, and pet expert second, I'm concerned about the cavalier (and I am not referring to the lovable purebred dog) attitude displayed by the media and many pet owners when it comes to the major responsibility of owning a dog. Despite all our anthropomorphizing, dogs are not human beings. And even though they're covered in fur, leather, or lace, they're not accessories. Unlike a fantastic pair of heels, dogs commit faux "paws." They bark at inappropriate times. They potty on the rug and unexpected places. They cause our significant others to have allergic reactions. They even get on people's nerves. In order to co-exist with them in our homes, dogs need health care, training, daily exercise, appropriate diet, grooming, and companionship.

So what if we do dress them well and wear matching outfits, buy them jewels, feed them gourmet food, bring them along on Take Your Dog to Work Day, display their pictures on our desks, and let them in our beds? We do these things because we love them and they become our family—especially for us single, upwardly mobile professionals with little time for a social life.

Most of us dog owners, however, appreciate our dogs as more than just style. They are superb companions. It is this social aspect of dog ownership that makes them such a great fit for our lifestyles and our society—they think of us as part of their pack and we think of them as part of our family.

C. R.

Index

Note: Bold page numbers indicate product resource guides.

Allergic reactions, 3, 32–33, **41**, 84, 85, **88**, 130–**31**, 177, 225–26

Allergies, dogs with, 68

Barking, 58–62

Baseball parks, 209–**16**
   fun and safety at, 211–14
   grooming and dressing for, 210–11
   pet games at, 214–15
   pre-game activities and attire, 210–11

Beach visits, 197–**202**
   dog beaches, 200
   environmental concerns, 199–200
   restrictions and leash laws, 197–99
   surfing, 201

Boarding kennels, 167–**74**
   dog at, 169–71
   finding and booking, 168–69
   returning home from, 171–73
   tipping practices, 172

Carriers (kennels), 92, **118**, 121, 183–84, 187–89, **195**

Children and dogs, 44–**49**
   older children helping train, 48–49
   showing children how to respond, 44–46
   teaching kids to communicate, 46–48

Clothes, costumes, and fashion, 15–19, 74, 75–81, 85–86, 211, 213

Crates, 59, 99, 129, 130, 176–77, 178, 194

Death and remembrance, 232–**38**
   burial/cremation options, 233–34, **237**
   euthanasia, 232–33
   memorials and grieving, 234–**38**

Delivery persons, dogs and, 61

Dental care, 14–15

Diet, 4
Divorce issues, 218–**23**
Dog parks/runs, 103–**8**
  gossiping at, 105–6
  paying attention at, 106
  rough play/fights at, 107–8
  social manners at, 104–5
  types of, 103–4
Dog walkers, 148

Eating habits, 21–**31**. *See also*
  Restaurants
  begging, 29–30
  controlling aggression, 27–28
  establishing routine, 26–27
  food/watering bowls and,
    25–26, 30
  stealing food, 22–25, **30–31**
Eating out, 119–**24**
Exercise, 4–5

First impressions, 2–3

Gifts, 65–**70**
  for dog lovers, 66
  for dogs, 66–**70**
  dogs as, 65–66
Groomers, 152–**59**
  appointments with, 155–58
  developing relationship
    with, 158–59

finding/making
  appointment, 153–55, **159**
what they do, 157–58
Grooming, 3–4, 9–15, **19**
  bathing, 13–14
  body maintenance, 12–13
  dental care, 14–15
  manicures and pedicures,
    10–11
  reducing allergens, 33
Guests, at your place, 32–**41**
  measures for them to take,
    39–40, 176–77
  preparing for, 32–34
  socializing dog and, 37–39
  training dog for, 34–37
Guests, you and dog as,
  176–**81**

Hotels, 190–91, 192–95

Leashes and collars, 17–18,
  34, 80, **88**, 93, **101**, **108**, 111,
  121, 198–99, **208**, **216**
Leash laws, 91

Multifamily living, 55–58

Neighborly actions, 50–**64**
  apartment elevators, 54–55
  barking, 58–62

city living, 53–55
controlling pet, 51–52
following community rules,
50–51
interviews for multi-family
buildings, 55–58
not imposing for sitting,
62–63
poop scooping, 50, 52–53,
64, 73, 91, 95
postal/delivery people and,
61

Park visits, 203–**8**
appropriate behavior, 206–7
planning and prepping,
205–6
state park treks, 203–5
Parties, 71–**81**
activities and food, 73–75, 81
costumes, 74, 75–81, 213
invitations, 72–73
location/guest list, 71–72
theme-specific, 75–81
Pet shuttles, 99
Poop scooping, 50, 52–53, **64**,
73, 91, 94–96, **101**
Postal workers, dogs and, 61
Product resources, **7–8**. *See
also specific topics*
Public transportation, 92

Relinquishing dogs, 224–**31**
avoiding, 224–26, **231**
finding new home or
shelter, 226–**31**
Restaurants, 119–**24**. *See also*
Eating habits
Retail establishments, 109–**18**
accidents in, 114–16
honoring pet policies,
109–11
pet strollers/carts in, 113–
14, **118**
resident pets in, 116–18
shopping together, 111–13,
115

Sitters, 62–63, 145–**51**
Socializing dog, 37–39, **41**

Tipping practices, xiii, 124,
148, 149, 158, 172
Trainers, 160–**66**
classes, 162–63
finding, with right program,
160–62, **166**
homework from, 163–64
staying in touch with,
164–65
Training, rewards of, 6–7
Training books, 5–6, **8**
Transportation options, 92, 99

Traveling, 182–**96**
air travel, 182–89, **195–96**
hotels, 190–91, 192–**95**
road trips, 189–92, **195–96**
you and dog as guests,
176–**81**

Veterinarians, 134–**44**
emergency protocol, 141
finding and choosing,
134–36
making appointments with,
136–37
office visits and exams,
137–41
payment terms, 142–43

Walking dog, 90–**102**
cell phones and, 96
common regulations, 91
crossing street, 100
dog walkers for, 148
as exercise, 93
following community rules,
90–91
leashes and, 93
meeting other dogs, 98–99
pooping and scooping,
94–96
talking to strangers and, 97
tying up and, 100

Wedding guests, dogs as,
82–**88**
getting permission, 83–84
health codes and, 87
incorporating into wedding,
82, 84–85, 86–87
outfits, 85–86
preparing dog, 84–85
rehearsal and special
considerations, 86–87
Weddings for dogs, 76–77
Work, dogs at, 125–**31**
benefits of, 125–26
comfort for all, 129–30
Dog to Work Day, 129,
239–40
getting permission, 126–28
prerequisites for, 128–29